"If you believe that people have no history worth mentioning, it's easy to believe they have no humanity worth defending."
— William Loren Katz

The Museum of disABILITY History's Classic Reprint Series

The Museum of disABILITY History's collections include a variety of books, magazines, documents, photographs and objects that help to illuminate the story of individuals with disabling conditions throughout the ages. The print materials from the Museum provide a snapshot of the tone and tenor of the times in regards to attitudes about and treatment of individuals with disabling conditions. Here is a classic article from the annals of disABILITY History.

PEOPLE INK PRESS

People Ink Press *in association with the* Museum of disABILITY History
3826 Main Street, Buffalo, New York 14226

A Poorhouse Trilogy

Questions Relating to Poorhouses,
Hospitals and Insane Asylums (1874)

Handbook for Visitors to the Poorhouse (1888)

He's Only a Pauper, Whom Nobody Owns! (1910)

Reprints from the Museum of disABILITY History Collection
Introduction by Douglas Farley

Publisher: Museum of disABILITY History

ISBN: 978-0-9893267-9-7
Library of Congress Control Number: 2015930860

People Ink Press
in association with the
Museum of disABILITY History
3826 Main Street
Buffalo, New York 14226

PEOPLE INK PRESS

Table of Contents

Introduction

By Douglas Farley, Director, Museum of disABILITY History

N ew York's history of caring for the poor, elderly, and disabled began while it was still a colony of the British Empire and continued throughout the twentieth century. A wide range of helping services and institutions were created, and some – under different names and settings – are still operating today. As societal needs and attitudes changed and knowledge evolved, many institutions merged, reorganized, or closed their doors forever.

In 1824 New York State established an almshouse law that required each county to build an almshouse or poorhouse to care for those who were unable to care for themselves. Almshouses – the first form of institutional help – typically cared for people who were poor, sick, homeless, mentally ill, injured, or considered mentally deficient. There were no specialized facilities such as nursing homes or institutions for people with special needs.

Through the work of the Museum of disABILITY History in Buffalo, New York, we bring to light the records and facilities of past helping programs that were abandoned with little documentation or local institutional memory. In the helping fields, care moves on. The past is quickly forgotten, often denied, and there is much easy criticism of previous efforts. This historical myopia leads to a narrow perspective as practices involving care and treatment evolve. Much of the historical research into earlier care in the almshouses, orphanages, and other institutions is negative. Early philosophies can seem dated and perhaps harsh, but at the time the care was given it was often the best available.

The Museum of disABILITY History and People Ink Press have combined three historic publications to create "A Poorhouse Trilogy." These three reprints include: "Questions Relating to Poorhouses, Hospitals and Insane Asylums" by John Ordronaux M.D. (State Charities Aid Association

Publication No. 3), 1874; "Handbook for the Visitors to the Poorhouse (1888)" by Frederick Law Olmsted; and "He's Only a Pauper, Whom Nobody Owns!" by James Oppenheim, written for the American Magazine, June 1910. We hope that this unique pairing of publications from the collection of the Museum of disABILITY History will provide a window in time to better understand the historical treatment of individuals with disabling conditions.

Allegany County Home, Angelica, New York

Chemung County Almshouse, New York

City Almshouse, Oswego, New York

County House, Breesport, New York

County House & Hospital, Ballston Spa, New York

County House, Delhi, New York

Erie County Alms House and Insane Asylum in Buffalo Plains, New York.

Greene County Alms House in Cairo, New York

Herkimer County House in Herkimer, New York

Lewis County Home in Lowville, New York

No. 19   Eaton—Madison County Home

Madison County Home in Eaton, New York

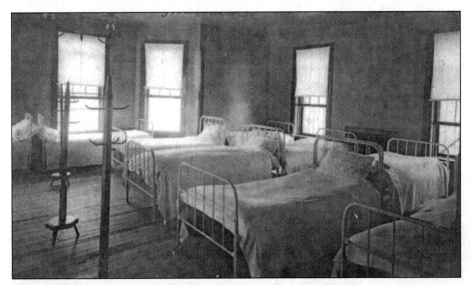

Madison County Home in Eaton, New York (sleeping quarters)

Niagara County Almshouse in Lockport, New York

Oneida County Home in Rome, New York

Oswego County Home in Mexico, New York

Poor House in Kingston, New York

chenectady's Public Buildings, County House

choharie County Alms House in Middleburg, New York

St. Lawrence County Alms House in Canton, New York

Suffolk County Alms House in Yaphank, Long Island

Wayne County Home in Lyons, New York

Chapter 1

Questions Relating to Poorhouses, Hospitals and Insane Asylums (1874)

Thee State Charities Aid Association, S.C.A.A., was founded in 1872. As its name connotes, the State Charities Aid Association's mission was to promote an active interest in New York State institutions of public charity, and aid the state in the administration of its public charities. It was organized as a nonprofit, nonsectarian, and independent organization and remains so today. The object of the State Charities Aid Association, which is a voluntary body of citizens of New York State, is to improve conditions in public institutions and to promote public health and child care. In its early years the association's purpose was to raise the awareness of the general public to the abuses and sufferings of paupers in the poor house system; to visit every institution of charity supported by public funds in the state of New York; to report findings of mismanagement and corruption, and to make recommendations to the State Commissioners of Public Charities (later renamed The State Board of Charities).

The State Charities Aid Association was started by pioneering social reformer Louisa Lee Schuyler in response to the deplorable conditions she observed in hospitals and almshouses in New York City. A great granddaughter of both General Phillip Schuyler and Alexander Hamilton, Schuyler used her social standing and keen organizational skills, honed by her Civil War relief efforts. Schuyler became interested in the problem of bad conditions in state poorhouses and almshouses after reading reports from the New York State Board of State Commissioners of Public Charities. She began organizing visiting committees of concerned citizens who would tour state institutions, make notes on what they saw, and act as advocates for improved conditions.

Advocating for changes in New York State legislation was a primary activity of SCAA from the start. The association helped to draft the first public health law and the first modern public welfare laws in New York State. In 1927 the Welfare Legislative Information Bureau (later the Legislative Information Bureau) was created to disseminate information about proposed legislation in SCAA's fields of interest to local SCAA committees and other interested organizations. SCAA advocated strongly for revision of the state constitution at the time of the Constitutional Convention in 1967, but proposed changes were never adopted.

For most of its history, SCAA was governed by a board of managers. Today the governing body is a board of trustees. During its earliest years, SCAA's reputation was bolstered by the service of numerous prominent New Yorkers on the board. These board members included Theodore Roosevelt, Elihu Root, Alfred E. Smith, Grace Dodge, Frederick Law Olmsted, Homer Folks and Henry Morgenthau.

In 1881, SCAA's visiting committees were legally guaranteed the right to inspect state facilities by the Right of Entrance Law. "Handbook for Visitors to the Poorhouse" was published following the initial inspections performed by the State Charities Aid Association. The initial inspections and findings would serve as a springboard for local groups of volunteer visitors interested in the inspection and improvement of prisons, poorhouses, workhouses, public hospitals, and schools. The goal of these groups was to form in each county a committee of citizen volunteers charged with visiting the county poorhouse, detecting and correcting abuses, securing the moral and physical welfare of the "inmates", and raising institutional standards of care. These citizen volunteers reported to the central association of members representing the most influential policymakers and reformers of the time. The book served as a guide to the volunteer visiting committees and provided uniformity in the reports and conclusions submitted.

No. 3.

State Charities Aid Association.

OFFICE,

52 EAST 20TH STREET,

New York.

QUESTIONS

RELATING TO

POORHOUSES, HOSPITALS AND INSANE ASYLUMS,

PREPARED FOR THE USE OF

VISITING COMMITTEES,

BY

JOHN ORDRONAUX M. D.

State Commissioner in Lunacy, Member State Board of Charities, Member State Charities
Aid Association.

February 1st. 1874.

New York :

CUSHING & BARDUA, STEAM BOOK AND JOB PRINTERS.
Nos. 128, 139, 141, 143 Centre Street.

QUESTIONS

FOR

VISITING COMMITTEES.

⸻ •◦• ⸻

The Secretaries of Visiting Committees are respectfully requested to obtain answers to the following questions through the Visitors, and to return one of the pamphlets with the blanks filled, by March 1st, addressed to the SECRETARY OF THE STATE CHARITIES AID ASSOCIATION, *52 East 20th Street*, NEW YORK.

LOUISA LEE SCHUYLER,

Pres't State Charities Aid Association.

Approved:

CHARLES S. HOYT,

Sec'y State Board of Charities.

February 1, 1874.

1st. When was the Hospital or Asylum built?

2d. Was it constructed for its present purpose?

3d. Have any changes ever been made in its architecture, whether internal or external?

4th. Are the walls solid?

Or have they an air space within or are they filled?

If so, with what?

5th. Are the outside walls,—if of brick or wood, painted?

If of stone, of what kind?

Limestone, sandstone, or granite?

6. Are the walls filled and plastered on the inner side?

Are they rough-cast or of hard finish?

How often are they lime washed?

How often are the ceilings lime washed?

7th. How are the floors scrubbed and with what?

Are they new and tight or old and cracked?

How often swept?

8th. How are the windows made to open?
Can they be lowered as well as raised?

How often are they opened?

Are they kept open at night?

Is the sun allowed to shine in freely every day wherever it can?

9th. Is there an infirmary for the sick?

On which floor is it situated?

On which side of the house, north or south, east or west?

Can the sun shine into it daily?

Are any trees very near to the walls on this side?

What are the cubic dimensions of this room and how many beds does it contain?

Are there any stables, piggeries, or barn-yards close to this side of the house?

10th. What is the system of ventilation in the building?

Natural or artificial?

Does it ever fail?

Is any bad odor ever perceptible in the halls, or, on stooping near the floor, in the morning?

11th. How often is the washing of clothes for the house done?

Where?

In the building or a separate house?

Are soiled clothes ever kept until a certain amount is accumulated before being washed?

If so, where?

12th. What is the method of heating?

If by stoves are they of cast or sheet-iron?

Is water ever kept upon them?

Is there any thermometer in the halls, and do the attendants govern the temperature by it?

13th. What is the cubic air space in each single bedroom?

What in each associated dormitory?

14th. What is the bedding?

Its amount and quality?

How often changed?

Are two persons ever put into one bed?

Have children beds separate from adults?

15th. Are any close stools or covered buckets provided for night use?

Any disinfectants ever used?

Are these buckets washed in hot water daily?

16th. How many attendants are there?

How many patients does each oversee?

17th. Do epileptics sleep in the same rooms and on the same kind of bedsteads as other patients?

18th. What is the clothing (upper and under) of patients?

Its amount, quality and when changed?

19th. How often do patients bathe?

Have they cold or warm water?

Soap and separate towels?

How often are their heads combed and washed?

Is their hair ever cut?

20th. What is the dietary? (Ask for a copy.)

Does it vary with the season?

Does it vary, at least at one meal daily?

Is butter ever omitted and molasses given in its stead?

What is the quality of the flour, butter, coffee, tea, sugar, potatoes, rice, etc. (Examine them.)

Which is most used, salt or fresh meat?

How often is pork used?

How often salt fish?

What are the vegetables used?

Any pickles ?

Is vinegar on the table daily,together with salt and pepper?

21st. Have the patients any occupation ?

Are they solicited or compelled to work ?

What work do they perform?

How many hours a day are they employed ?

Are they ever punished?

If so, in what way ?

22d. Is there any airing or exercise ground for those who need fresh air, yet cannot work ?

23d. Are there any trees close to the buildings ?

If so, of what kind ?

Evergreen or deciduous ?

Is the ground wet about the building ?

What is the soil, clay or sand?

What is the drainage, surface or artificial ?

Is *mould* common indoors?

Are cess-pools used, or are there drains to carry off kitchen slops?

24th. Are any basements used as bed-rooms, or punishment cells or day rooms?

25th. Are any amusements provided for the patients?

26th. Can friends visit them, or bring any suitable delicacies?

27th. Does any Physician reside in the House?

If not, how near is he?

Does one visit it regularly, or only upon call?

28th. Has there been any sickness in the House?

If so, what was it?

How often has it appeared and how long did it last?

Was it limited to any particular part of the house?

How many Deaths during the past month?

From what cause?

29th. What was the number of patients received during the past month ?

How many discharged ?

30th. Who superintends the House ?

Any assistant ?

Has the superintendent any other occupation ?

31st. Is any farm attached to the Institution ?

Is its produce consumed on the premises, or sold ?

What is the estimated value of the farm produce ?

Chapter 2

Handbook for Visitors to the Poorhouse (1888)

B orn in Hartford, Connecticut, in 1822. Between 1837 and 1857, Frederick Law Olmsted performed a variety of jobs: he was a clerk, a sailor in the China trade, and a farmer, as well as many other professions. He moved to New York in 1848 and in 1857, without having ever had any college education, Olmsted became the superintendent of New York's Central Park.

As the superintendent of the park he served as the administrator and then architect-in-chief of Central Park's construction. Next, he served as the administrative head of the US Sanitary Commission, which was the forerunner of the American Red Cross. Finally his last job, before forming his own firm, was that of the manager of the vast Mariposa gold mining estate in California.

In addition to designing for urban life, Olmsted was anxious to preserve areas of natural beauty for future public enjoyment. He served as the first head of the commission in charge of preserving Yosemite Valley and was a leader in establishing the Niagara Reservation, which he planned with Calvert Vaux, in 1887.

Between 1872 and 1895, when he retired, Olmsted's firm carried out 550 projects. These projects included college campuses, the grounds to the US Capitol, and residential communities. In late 1895 he suffered a mental breakdown and spent his remaining years resting in an Asylum in Waverly, Massachusetts. He died in August 1903. It was not until 20 years later that people began to realize the impact and grandness of Olmsted's work, and the vast wonders that he left the world.

No. 12

STATE CHARITIES AID ASSOCIATION

Hand-Book for Visitors

TO

THE POORHOUSE

FOURTH EDITION, REVISED AND CORRECTED

NEW YORK AND LONDON

G. P. PUTNAM'S SONS

1888

Edited by a special committee, Frederick Law Olmsted,
Chairman. Adopted by the State Charities Aid Association,
November 9, 1876. Revised by a special committee,

January 1888.

STATE CHARITIES AID ASSOCIATION
21 UNIVERSITY PLACE, NEW YORK

OFFICERS, 1887-'88

PRESIDENT	*TREASURER*
Mr. J. HAMPDEN ROSS	Mr. CHARLES RUSSELL HONE
VICE-PRESIDENT	*SECRETARY*
Dr. CHARLES HITCHCOCK	Mr. WYLLYS HODGES

LIBRARIAN
MISS A. H. WOOLSEY
21 University Place

BOARD OF MANAGERS

Miss ELEANOR BLODGETT	Miss S.E. MINTON
Miss ROSALIE BUTLER	Mr. J. HAMPDEN ROBB
Prof. THEODORE W. DWIGHT	Miss LOUISA LEE SCHUYLER
Dr. CHARLES HITCHCOCK	Mr. W. A. W. STEWART
Mr. CHARLES RUSSELL HOWE	Mrs. MERRITT TRIMBLE
Mr. HENRY E. HOWLAND	Mr. HORACE WHITE
Mr. JOHN A. McKIM	Miss A. H. WOOLSEY

Dr. W. GILL WYLIE

CONTENTS

PART I.—PRELIMINARY ADVICE

PART II.—MATTERS IN GENERAL

PART III.—THE SICK

1. Accommodations for the sick.
2. Contagious wards.
3. Maternity rooms.
4. Laundry for Infirmary.
5. Sanitary cleanliness.
6. Ventilation.
7. Disinfection.
8. Beds and bedding.
9. Diet.
10. Hired nurse.

PART IV.—AGED AND INFIRM

1. Duty of support by relatives.
2. Quarters, clothing, spectacles, books, etc.

PART V.—BLIND, AND DEAF AND DUMB

1. Provisions for, out of Poorhouse.
2. Their special claims.
3. Employment.
4. Education of the Blind.
5. Education of the Deaf and Dumb.

PART VI.—INSANE AND IDIOTIC

1. Classification of the Insane.
2. State provision for acute cases.
3. State provision for chronic cases.
4. Early stage of Insanity.
5. Dietary for the Insane.
6. Occupations.
7. Quarters.
8. Attendants.
9. Cleanliness, clothing, and bed-covering.
10. Protest against the retention of the Insane in Poorhouses.
11. Idiotic children.

PART VII.—ABLE-BODIED PAUPERS

1. The rule which should govern their admission.
2. Employment: (to be systematic, not optional).
3. Applicants through misfortune.
4. Employment for such to be looked for out of the Poorhouse.
5. Political patronage to be avoided.

PART VIII.—CHILDREN

1. The law and its motives.
2. Hereditary pauperism.
3. Finding Homes.
4. Infirm children in the Poorhouse.
5. Their rooms, chairs, tables.
6. Out-door life, companions, and occupations.
7. Cleanliness and ventilation.
8. Clothing.
9. Sleeping.

APPENDIX.

A. Notes on Disinfection.
B. Law as to the Care of Relatives.
C. Law as to the Removal of Children from the Poorhouse.
D. Diet and Care of Children.
E. Law Conferring upon the State Charities Aid Association the Power to Inspect Poorhouses, etc.
F. Draft of Constitution for Local Visiting Committees.
G. Additional Suggestions and Information for Visiting Committees.

HAND-BOOK FOR VISITORS TO THE POORHOUSE.

PART I.

PRELIMINARY ADVICE.

1. This hand-book presents under various heads, memoranda which may be useful to a Visiting Committee.*

In opening it, a word of caution may be needed against the presumption that members of the committee should be experts in Poorhouse management.

A conviction that the community is ignorant and indifferent as to what goes on in the Poorhouse is at the root of all that is wrong. Every visit, therefore, which gives the impression that a sincere and lasting interest is taken in the welfare of its inmates, will tend to reform all its evils. A clear perception of each of them, and a readiness to prescribe at once a remedy, are by no means necessary.

What is chiefly to be desired, as a preparation for the work, is a disposition to be thoroughly and in the best sense charitable, not only toward paupers, but toward those charged with their care.

Such a disposition will be fostered by the reflection that the standard of duty which exists in the minds of all the officials of the Poorhouse, is one to which they have been educated, and that the community can not rightfully expect a better class of services than it systematically calls for, and willingly pays for at the market rate, or in other' words, than public opinion demands in a persistent and practical, not simply in a spasmodic, occasional and sensational way.

---

*It is the aim of the State Charities' Aid Association, to organize Visiting Committees for every county of the State of New York. In those counties where Visiting Committees do not already exist, persons desirous of forming themselves into committees are requested to communicate with the Secretary of the Association, who will furnish a plan of organization (see Appendix F).

2. On the organization of a Visiting Committee,* its executive committee should officially call on the Superintendents of the Poor, and explain the nature of the proposed undertaking.

Every care should be taken to make them understand that the work of the Committee is intended and is likely, to be a help and not a hindrance to them, and that the difficulties with which they have to contend and which stand in the way of improvements and reforms are fully recognized.

Pleasant personal relations with the keeper of the Poorhouse, and with all the attendants, will make the work of the Committee much more agreeable and useful than it could otherwise be.

---

3. It should be arranged that (besides occasional unexpected calls) there should be regular and stated visits to the Poorhouse at certain fixed intervals. The more frequent they can be made without over taxing the strength of the Committee the better, but no plan should be adopted which cannot surely be carried out with punctuality and exactness. In this respect the committee should be an example of system and discipline to the officials.

A record should be kept and an entry invariably made of the date and the observations of each visit.

The more full and exact the minutes of visits can be made, without an excessive expenditure of time, the better; for it is impossible to anticipate the bearing or the value which any entry may afterward come to have as evidence.

*See Appendix G, 1-4 inclusive.

4. In cases where, after a course of patient and cautious investigation, a Superintendent or other officer is found beyond question dishonest, unscrupulous or grossly inefficient, a careful statement of the important facts of the case should be prepared and published and an energetic, persevering agitation begun for the removal of the offender.*

Unless, however, positive offenses can be clearly proved, it will be generally better to avoid such a course, and it is always well to remember that when a removal shall have been accomplished, the successor may turn out to be no better than the man thrown out.

Nor should the fact be forgotten that experience in public office necessarily carries with it a certain amount of knowledge which a fresh incumbent must lack, and a power of' usefulness which, if it can by any means be rightly directed, may be of much value.

For this and other reasons the influence of the Committee should, as a general rule, be favorable to the retention of keepers, matrons and other subordinates who seem to be moderately well qualified for their duties, and in all cases opposed to changes of which the motive is one of political patronage.

---

5. It will be observed that the more definite advice to visitors which follows is mainly confined under all its various heads to matters of physical welfare. This is partly because the mental and moral improvement of paupers greatly depends upon, and will generally follow, the reforms therein suggested, and partly because it is impossible to give specific directions for dealing with souls as with bodies.

*See Appendix G, 3·

We can classify and control the physical by general rules to a certain and most important extent, but our effect upon the spiritual condition of those we seek to aid must be, for the most part, individual, and will vary with every case brought before us.

And yet every life with which the visitors will come in contact at the Poorhouse is necessarily a broken one, probably a wasted and hopeless one, made so by the fault, by the sin of the sufferers themselves, or by that of those with whom they are connected, and it is the highest office of the visitors to show to these poor forlorn fellow-beings that their life, even in a Poorhouse, may have its use and its beauty; that they also, bruised and shattered as they are, can help their fellow sufferers, can comfort the broken-hearted, can, while exercising self-control over their own evil tendencies, strengthen the weaker to good resolutions and hold up the hands of those who have even a harder battle to fight than themselves.

Among the inmates of every Poorhouse will be found those who come in "for the winter," and who will probably return to it every year, until some day they come to stay, and die.

These can, perhaps, be inspired with fresh hope, can be helped with work and counsel, can be encouraged to struggle through the next hard season without recourse to public charity, and may thus recover their independence and self-respect. A little wise help may sometimes save whole families from permanent pauperism.

Finally the visitors will always bear in mind that by the presentation of a high ideal of goodness, charity and truth, a powerful influence can not fail to be exerted upon the unfortunate inmates of the Poor house, and that by direct and indirect means they may be drawn to take a higher view of their duty to themselves and their fellows.

PART II.

MATTERS IN GENERAL.

1. There should be an absolute and entire separation of the male and female inmates of the Poor house, not only in the living rooms, but in the halls, stairways, dining-room and yards.

Persons of good character forced to take refuge in the Poorhouse by infirmities should not be compelled to associate closely with the vicious and degraded.*

Imperfect arrangements in these two particulars will be found fruitful of obstacles to good management in all others. They should, therefore, have the earliest and most careful consideration of the Committee.

---

2. Next in importance will be the rules with respect to personal cleanliness, and the neatness, good order and purity of the air of the buildings and their appurtenances.

All that can be gained with respect to these will have a twofold advantage, directly in the improved health of the paupers; indirectly in the effect on their dispositions and habits. Order and neatness suggest and demand the exercise of prudence and painstaking, and can only be

*See note, p. 28.

maintained by a close scrutiny of details and an adherence to method which will be favorable to good management in all particulars.

A systematic search for defects in cleanliness and purity of air should therefore be made at every visit, and within regular periods should cover every part of the Poorhouse, its furniture, outhouses and grounds.

The observations which immediately follow relate more particularly to this part of the Committee's duty, in which good housekeepers will find their ordinary habits come directly and most usefully into play.

---

3.   Water-closets, cellars, garrets and all places which are liable to be the receptacles of disused furniture, musty barrels and the like, should be closely, watched. Danger always lurks in decaying wood. The windows of such places should as much as practicable be kept open, and their walls frequently whitewashed. Neglect in these particulars is often the cause of a foulness in the air pervading a whole building.

Bath-tubs, basins, faucets, pumps and tubs should be often examined, and it should be seen whether plenty of water, soap, combs, brushes and towels are provided.

The supply of water should be equal to six gallons daily for each inmate, and it is best as a general rule that each should, besides ordinary partial ablutions daily, be given a full bath once a week. The practice may prevail, and should be watched against, of washing either clothes or dishes in the bath-tubs.

Basements and cellars of dwellings should not be used for the storage of roots, fruits or vegetables. They should be kept dry and ventilated. No part of a basement should be used for bedrooms, day rooms or punishment cells.

4. The method of heating the building should be attended to. Sometimes the rooms will be found so cold as to cause suffering, sometimes so hot as to be weakening. From 68° to 70° Fahr. will be best for the greater number.

The ventilation of the rooms is a matter of the highest importance, almost always neglected by ignorant persons. The tops of the windows should be kept open as much as possible, and there should be ventilators over the doors of the rooms and in the upper part of the windows.

---

5. There should be a separate bed for each in mate. Putting two persons in one bed or three in two placed close together is a very bad practice.

Sheets and blankets should be aired daily and beds frequently made over with new straw.

Vessels of water should be kept on stoves to prevent excessive dryness of the heated air.

---

6. The yards and grounds about the house should be conveniently arranged and provided with walks and seats, so that the inmates may with advantage be generally required to spend considerable time every day out of doors.

To this end a certain number of shaded benches are desirable, as well as others in protected and sunny positions to which the old and feeble may resort in damp and chilly weather.

The grounds should be well drained and neatly kept, the walks daily swept and the turf mown at frequent intervals and kept clear of weeds.

If trees are wanting they should be carefully planted where they will not shade the house, and when planted should be protected from injury.

Stables, piggeries, etc., should be at a distance from the house; if too near, the evil may be reduced to moderate proportions, by due care in their management.

A bad smell is sure evidence that this is lacking. If it comes from a manure heap, an occasional layer of dry earth is a cheap preventive. As a more available means of immediate relief from a nuisance, a solution of copperas in water, or plaster of Paris applied as a dry powder (as sold for agricultural use) may be recommended.*

---

7. Such evils as have thus far been referred to (imperfect classification arid separation, impurity of air, and general untidiness}, will commonly be alleged by those in charge of a Poorhouse, to be a necessary result of insufficient and faulty buildings.

As to lack of room, simply, if a strict examination of all applicants for admission, and the rejection of all to whom it is not due, can be secured, the need for crowding will in most cases be much abated.

If, however, the buildings are decidedly inadequate and unsuitable, the superintendents and super visors should, if possible, be brought to realize the necessity for improvements. If they continue long neglectful in the matter, a discussion of the subject may be begun in the county newspaper, which should be followed up steadily and judiciously till the public mind sufficiently understands the false economy of their course, when petitions favoring the necessary changes may be prepared and the county canvassed for signatures.

As soon as it is determined to build a new Poor house, or to make important additions to an old one, the Committee is requested to inform the Association of the fact, when special advice on the subject and plans will be provided.

*Various methods of disinfection, are given in the Appendix, (A).

---

8.   However unsuitable the buildings may be, the Committee should, by shrewd, patient and resolute efforts, seek to stimulate a disposition to make the best of them while their use continues.

With careful study of all the circumstances the Committee may be able to devise and carry out expedients by which real difficulties will be lessened and plausible excuses for certain defects wholly removed.

If the officers of the Poorhouse are favorably disposed, many little improvements in the buildings and grounds may be gradually accomplished with but slight outlays, and, possibly, without special appropriations, the aggregate result of which, through the better tone of management to which they will insensibly lead, will amply reward much patient labor.

With regard to such incidental improvements the Committee may be reminded that fitness, propriety, congruity and substantial refinement in material things tend to the like conservative and orderly qualities in the .minds of those habituated to them and may be assured that means to secure them in and about the Poorhouse are as strictly utilitarian and economical as those for saving food, fuel or lights.

Among expedients of the sort above referred to some of the following may be found available.

Sheds, bins and close yards for the deposit of rubbish and the compact and cleanly storage of materials before scattered and encumbering the grounds.

Pegs, racks, shelves and closets within the house, with the like object.

The subdivision of yards by fences to secure a proper classification, and the separation of different classes, of the inmates of the house.

Changes in the lines of lanes or routes of transportation by which grounds may be enlarged or their awkward division and littering may be avoided. The removal or setting back of fences, with like objects.

The use of flag, brick, gravel or plank on the surface of walks liable to be muddy.

The furnishing of doorways with scrapers and mats.

The thorough under-drainage of damp yards with open-jointed tile or broken stone. (Such drains may be three feet deep and 25 feet apart.)*

Leading drains from cellars where water is liable to accumulate after severe storms. (Care should be taken that their place of outflow is not a cesspool or other source of foul air.)

Where buildings are under a hill or on sloping ground, making catch-water drains above them, by which flooding of the surface of the yards may be prevented.

The substitution for sluggish surface ditches of underground conduits, or neat gutters paved or with long sodded slopes which may be kept smooth and clean with the scythe and rake.

The substitution of open fire-places or "Franklins" for air-tight, cylinder, or other forms of stoves.

In any large, much occupied room when heated by steam or hot water pipes or hot air furnaces, a great improvement in the quality of the air can generally be effected by keeping even a very small open fire in it. A "Franklin" may be generally introduced for the purpose without great inconvenience or expense.

Drafts from doors and windows, intolerable to old and rheumatic people, may be often avoided by a tube bringing air from the outside near to the mouth of stoves or fireplaces. If on the lower floor, the tube may be carried through the basement. For an ordinary large Franklin stove a tube of boards, 8 by 3 inches will answer. A hole in the floor of the same size, just in front of the hearth, will admit the air. This may be covered by an iron register, or a wooden box open on the side toward the fire.

Smoking chimneys may sometimes be relieved by the expedient last suggested; sometimes by increasing the length of flues by chimney pots or building the chimney higher; sometimes by topping them with cowls: often, however, the difficulty is radical in the form of the chimney and nothing expensive should be urged except under advice of a responsible architect.

In furnace-heated rooms the air is often fouler than is necessary on account of the absence or the insufficient size of the air-supply duct, or because the air which enters it comes from a bad locality. Such ducts, if made of boards and carried along the ceiling of the basement, can be enlarged and extended at small cost.

Dark and close passages may be made more wholesome and cheerful by the introduction of windows, or lights in doors or transoms; by whitewashing walls, or by the substitution of open trellis-work for close boarding.

*For full advice as to this matter see a small book by Waring, *Drainage for Health and Drainage for Profit*, and as to house drainage, a larger book by the same author, *The Sanitary Drainage of Houses and Towns*.

Belts of coniferous trees may be planted to lessen the force of harsh winds, (the common white pine will generally be best), and scattered trees to relieve bareness and bleakness.

Old walls, fences or other unsightly objects may be hidden by vines or by screens of shrubs or of strong, coarse, herbaceous plants, such as sunflowers, castor bean or Indian corn. Beds of flowers may in some cases be planted with advantage to relieve the gloom of a yard.

Old and partially disabled people among the paupers may be given an agreeable occupation in making many such improvements as have been suggested. But whenever cheap expedients are to be used, care should be taken that the promised advantage from them is not lost by over-slight work or subsequent neglect. Firmness, neatness and orderliness are to be aimed at in all rather than prettiness or picturesqueness.

---

9. Another matter requiring the systematic attention of the Committee will be the food of the paupers.

This should be wholesome as to the quality of the raw material, suitably cooked, carefully varied and reasonably abundant.

The meals should be neatly served, at regular hours, and cleanly habits should be required at table. The use of knives and forks and of cups (instead of pans) is essential to such habits.

The usual "house diet" should consist of beef or mutton, with potatoes and bread, for at least four days in the week, and soup with vegetables on the alternate days. Often in Poorhouses pork (salted) is almost the only meat used. Juicy vegetables, pickles and vinegar are necessary to health. Tea or rye coffee should be given every morning and night, and wheat and Graham bread should be alternated with well cooked hominy and oatmeal.

10. Another matter to be looked to by the Committee is that of clothing. The probability is that it will not be sufficient either for the comfort or the cleanliness of the paupers.

The supply of underclothing should be ample, and changed at regular times, washed every week and when washed mended, before being put away and locked up.

All the paupers should have nightclothes and not be allowed to sleep in garments worn by day.

Pains should be taken to keep all clothing which is the private property of the inmates apart from the common stock.

A suitable supply of bedding should be kept on hand and in good condition and visitors should frequently observe whether the inmates, especially the old and infirm, have sufficient covering to keep them warm.

———————

11. A Sunday school will prove a pleasure to most of the inmates, old and young. It is desirable that regular religious services be provided, in which singing and reading should be important parts. Without effort to prevent it, Sunday will commonly be a longer, blanker day than any other.

A daily school in the Poorhouse is also desirable. All its inmates will be the better for some intellectual training, and one or two hours of schooling each day may with advantage be made generally obligatory.

———————

12. A library should be collected in every Poorhouse. The sick and disabled can while away many weary hours with a book. On Sunday especially all should have pleasant reading. The library should be kept locked and the key left in the charge of some competent person who would change the books once a week, and see that none were injured or lost. The books should be neatly covered and labeled.

The visitors will find themselves much more welcome if they make a practice of reading aloud in the sick room and many useful lessons could be given in this way.

---

13. A burial service should be performed for each inmate who dies in the Poorhouse, and there should be a separate grave and proper registry of death.

---

14. If the visitors report an appearance of undue extravagance in the management of the Poorhouse, it will of course be the duty of the Committee to inquire into the matter, and when they are sure of the facts, and have called the attention of the Superintendents to them without effect, then to make them public.

The contrary fault will, however, be found more common, viz., a penurious economy in providing food, clothing and attendants, and the Committee will have accomplished a great deal when it has convinced the Superintendents that a want of wisdom in saving often defeats its end, and is as bad a fault as careless expenditure.

If saving is to be the sole object, the best method of dealing with the poor is not to provide for them at all.

The letter from a lady, in the appendix, on the care of infants, contains many suggestions of value, applicable to the general management of the Poorhouse.

NOTE.-To prevent the further degradation of the younger women in Poorhouses and Jails, by association with persons more hardened and vicious than themselves, a Reformatory for Women has been established by appropriation from the State, at Hudson, N.Y. It is designed to receive women between the ages of fifteen and thirty, convicted before a magistrate of misdemeanor. Members of Visiting Committees may be able to bring about the removal to this Institution of such women as seem to them to be fit subjects for reformatory treatment.

PART III.

THE SICK.

1. Every Poorhouse should have its infirmary. For the smallest, at least two rooms are indispensable, one for men and one for women, between which there should be no communication.

It is much better that the infirmary should stand well apart from buildings for all other purposes.

When any alterations or additions are to be made, or new structures erected for the sick, the Committee is requested to communicate with the Association, when advice will be given as to plans for both large and small hospitals and hospital arrangements which will insure both economy and efficiency of management.

---

2.   Infectious and contagious diseases should always be provided for in buildings standing apart from those for the other sick or the well.

If special buildings are lacking when such diseases make their appearance, there can hardly be a better place for them than a tent.

The following is a description of a cottage built for the accommodation of infectious cases by the trustees of the Presbyterian Hospital in New York, from plans furnished by the State Charities Aid Association.

"The cottage stands on locust posts a foot high, the space under it having been excavated ten inches, and filled in with ashes and concrete. It consists of one room, twenty feet square, with two beds for patients, and one for a nurse, screened off by a wooden partition, which includes one of the windows. The windows are five feet by three and of good quality of glass and the building has light and air on all four sides. The roof, walls and floor are double, and the interspace is ventilated by means of hinged boards, opening outwards at the top and bottom of the outer wall. The upper floor is of Georgia pine, well laid. Between the floors run tin extraction tubes for drawing the foul air away from the room. A register opens under each bed, and the flues unite in a drum behind the stove, which is an open Franklin. The stove-pipe is double, the inner smoke flue warming the space- between and making an aspirating chimney on a small scale. This arrangement has been perfectly successful. Fresh air descends into the room through air-boxes which reach from the roof below the level of the eaves, and are fitted with an adjustable scatter-plate at their mouths. There are also transoms over the door and windows to assist in ventilation. The cottage was tested for the first time during the heavy storm of February [1876] when the minimum Fahrenheit outside was 7°; and after the first day or two, being then thoroughly warmed and dried, it was kept comfortable with a temperature ranging from 65° to 75°, day and night, and the air was always clean and good. The cost of the building complete, without furniture was $279."

---

3. Maternity cases should be as carefully isolated as the most infectious; at least a room should be prepared for them separate from all others. No more than three such cases should be allowed together.

The best place for a maternity ward, if a separate building cannot be afforded for the purpose, will be in an upper story, because proper ventilation can there be better commanded. It is of the greatest importance, however, when so situated, that there should be no surgical cases in the rooms below.

A much better arrangement is to provide a cottage similar to that just recommended for infectious cases; still better, if the number of cases justifies the outlay, two cottages to be used alternately.

A nurse when in charge of a lying-in room should not be allowed to attend surgical or medical patients. All inmates save those connected with this department should be denied access to it.

---

4.   There should be a separate laundry for the hospital and no clothes or bedding which have been used by patients should be washed in the Poorhouse. A shed in the yard will commonly be best for the purpose.

---

5.   The Committee's inspection as to the cleanliness and purity of the air of the Poorhouse, should of course be specially thorough in all that pertains to the infirmary.

It should be seen that there are at least four clean towels provided every week for each patient, and an extra one for the weekly bath.

Hospital utensils should be of earthenware rather than of tin.

The space under the beds should be perfectly clean and free for the circulation of air. The patients' boxes and belongings should be provided for elsewhere.

The water-closets, sinks, bed-pans and all other visible appurtenances of the hospital being found thoroughly clean, if the air is perceptibly impure, the plumbing and drains should be examined by an expert.

6.   In all the rooms the windows should open easily at the top, and as many through draughts be established as possible without chilling the patients. Perforated zinc plates should be placed in front of all upper sashes.

Whenever any ward is unoccupied, all the windows and doors should be kept wide open, in winter as well as in summer, extremes of heat and cold being the best disinfectants.

---

7.   All garments and bedding used by patients should be thoroughly disinfected before being again used. After infectious diseases they should be burnt outside the premises.*

---

8.   Bedsteads should be of iron, painted green and washed once a month or oftener.

Beds should be regularly emptied at the death or departure of each patient, the straw, which is by far the best filling, burned, the ticks scalded, well washed and refilled.

Bed linen and clothing should be changed often enough to keep the patients always comfortably clean, and sheets and blankets frequently aired.

Blankets require frequent washing.

Care is needed that the bed linen and the garments of the patients be perfectly dry when used.

There should be a good supply of warm coverings for winter. Woolen blankets are much better than "comfortables."

*See appendix A.

9. The sick should always receive more careful attention as to diet than is required for the inmates in general, and it must be borne in mind that the object is to cure them as quickly as possible.

The proper food for them includes beef-tea, butter, milk, eggs, beefsteak, tea and toast.

All meals, except for patients too ill to sit up, should be served in the infirmary dining-room, and eating not allowed in the wards.

A vigilant visitor will occasionally and unexpectedly drop in at dinner time to see that the dining room service, table cloths, dishes, spoons, knives and. forks are clean and sufficient, that the food is of good quality and that the patients in bed get their meals hot and comfortably served; also that the physician's orders with regard to special diet are strictly carried out.

———————

10. No feeble, intemperate or disabled person should be allowed to attend on the sick, and there should always be at least one good paid nurse in every Poorhouse.

PART IV.

AGED AND INFIRM.

1. These, who may be considered as permanent inmates of the Poorhouse, have often been compelled to seek refuge under its inhospitable roof by no fault of their own, and, as many years may elapse before death comes to give them release, every alleviation of their hard lot, consistent with the duty owed to the tax-payers by those to whom the trust of expending the public moneys has been confided, should be encouraged.

But the visitors should especially inquire if such inmates have no relatives able to support them in whole or in part, and who, in such case, are bound by law to do so.* If it be found that there are such relatives living in the State, they should be called upon to perform their duty, and in case of refusal, should be compelled to do so. It is the acknowledged duty of children to provide for those who, when they had strength, toiled for, and supported them, but the feeling of this duty is often blunted by the facility with which public aid is granted in such cases.

* See Appendix B.

2.   Respectable old people, who have known better days, and who have been brought to the Poorhouse by loss of children, illness or other misfortunes, should not be compelled to associate with the vicious and degraded.

In some cases it may be practicable to put two old women or two old men in a small room by themselves, where they can have some home feeling and sense of privacy.

It should always be remembered that in the aged, the blood circulates poorly, and that they require to be kept in a warmer temperature than younger and stronger persons. They often suffer from rheumatism and need woolen clothing even in warm weather.

Old people should be provided with suitable spectacles, that they may be able to read and sew.

Picture books, illustrated papers, checkers and other simple games will help them to pass the time.

Reading to them will often give great pleasure.

The old women will like to knit and make patchwork.

PART V.

BLIND AND DEAF AND DUMB.

1. The State provides for all children of sound mind of these classes elsewhere than in the Poorhouse, as will be more fully stated later. With regard to all others, as has been said of the aged, it is of the first importance that they should not be admitted to the Poorhouse, or retained in it, except on grounds of stem necessity.

---

2. Where, however, those of maturer years have no relatives who can be required or prevailed upon to provide for them elsewhere, it should be recognized that more properly than any others they are entitled to seek special aid of the public. They should, therefore, be guarded against a sense of degradation in accepting whatever of comfort the Poorhouse can give them, and should be made to feel as little as possible of the hardness which must as a rule be expected to attend the systematic administration of charity.

---

3. More to them perhaps than to any others, the best form of charity is that by which they may be lifted in a measure above charity, through occupations in which they can be useful to others and have the satisfaction and moral profit of more or less paying their own way.

In searching for such employments, it should not be forgotten that both the Blind and the Deaf and Dumb may possess, and like to display, a degree of strength and activity rarely found among the proper inmates of the Poorhouse, and that their self-respect may often, also, be safely gratified by trusts which could not be properly given to paupers who have become such through their own moral feebleness.

---

4.   There are two Institutions in the State for the education of the blind, viz:

The New York Institution for the Blind, at New York City;
The New York State Institution for the Blind, at Batavia.

Each is strictly educational in its objects, and serves in no way as an asylum or hospital for the cure of blindness.

Beyond the ordinary means of public school instruction, however, these institutions provide for the training of the blind in various useful callings.

Except in special cases, pupils are admitted to them from eight to twenty-one years of age, and may remain as long as shall be thought advisable in each case by the Board of Trustees.

The institution in New York receives pupils from the counties of New York, Kings, Queens and Suffolk; the institution at Batavia from the remaining fifty-six counties of the State.

Applications for admission may be made by any relative or friend, or by the Supervisors of the county, to the Superintendents of these Institutions.

Pupils chargeable to the State are supported by an annual appropriation from the State. The charges for clothing and traveling expenses are paid by the counties to which the pupils belong, and must never exceed $60 per year for each.

5.   There are seven institutions in the State for the education of the Deaf and Dumb, viz.;

The New York Institution for the Deaf and Dumb, New York City;
The Central New York Institution for Deaf Mutes, Rome;
Institution for the Improved Instruction of Deaf Mutes,
    New York City;
The Western New York Institution for Deaf Mutes, Rochester;
The Northern New York Institution for Deaf-Mutes, Malone;
Le Couteulx St. Mary's Deaf and Dumb Asylum, Buffalo.;
St. Joseph's Institution for Deaf-Mutes, Brooklyn.

These institutions are open to all Deaf and Dumb residents of the State, of suitable age and capacity.

The law directs that when a Deaf and Dumb child between the ages of six and twelve becomes a charge for its maintenance on any of the towns or counties, the Overseer of the Poor of the town or the Supervisor of the county shall place such child in one of the institutions in the State for the education of Deaf-Mutes. Children placed in such institutions are required to be maintained at the expense of the county to which they belong, such expense never to exceed $300 each per year for board, tuition, and clothing.

The Western New York Institution charges only $250 per annum for its county pupils, and makes the charge of $300 for the clothing of State pupils only when the expenditure seems to warrant it.

Deaf and Dumb persons between the ages of twelve and twenty-five are received at the same institutions, provided their application be approved by the Superintendent of Public Instruction at Albany. Such application may be made by the nearest relative or friend, or by the

Supervisor of the county. They are then State pupils, and the charge for their board and tuition, $300 each per year, is paid by the State.

A charge of $30 per year is made to the county for the clothing of the State pupils.

The regular term for such pupils is five years, but the Superintendent of Public Instruction may at his discretion extend the term of any pupil for a period not exceeding three years.

At the institution for the Improved Instruction of Deaf Mutes in New York City children are not received if over fourteen, the object of the institution being exclusively to teach articulation. In the other institutions, various useful trades are taught.

These institutions have no special district, but receive pupils from all the counties of the State.

PART VI.

INSANE AND IDIOTIC.

1. The State makes special provision for Insane and Idiotic paupers.

For the Insane, there are two classes of Asylums, one for acute cases and one for chronic cases. The law defines acute cases as those where the disease is of less than one year's duration; chronic cases as those where the disease has continued for one or more years.

---

2. The law directs the County Superintendents of the Poor, to send all cases of acute insanity, charge able to the town or county, within ten days to one of the State Lunatic Asylums, except in the counties of New York, Kings and Monroe. These counties are authorized by special law to take charge of their own cases of acute insanity.

The State Lunatic Asylums for the treatment of acute cases are four in number, viz:

New York State Lunatic Asylum, Utica;
Hudson River State Hospital, Poughkeepsie;
Buffalo State Asylum for the Insane, Buffalo;
State Homeopathic Asylum for the Insane, Middletown.

A fifth Asylum is being erected at Ogdensburgh, but it is not expected that even with this added capacity the State Asylums can furnish room for all of the insane in the State, and it is hoped that further provision will be made for them.

---

3. The law directs that all cases of chronic insanity* be sent to the Willard Asylum at Ovid, except from the following counties, which are allowed to take care of their own chronic insane : New York, Kings, Monroe, and Clinton, exempted from the operation of the Willard Asylum act by a special act of the Legislature; Broome, Cattaraugus, Chautauqua, Chenango, Cortland, Erie, Jefferson, Lewis, Oneida, Onondaga, Orange, Oswego, Queens, Suffolk, Tioga, Ulster, Wayne, and Wyoming, exempted by action of the State Board of Charities. These counties are required to make special provision for the care of their chronic insane. If they do not make such provision the State Board of Charities can revoke the authority given to them. There should be, in each of these counties, proper buildings for the purpose, with well paid physicians and attendants who are experts in the care of the Insane. Dr. Ordronaux, the State Commissioner in Lunacy, in his report for 1874 says:-" No insane person should be kept in any Poorhouse unless it has a special department for that purpose equipped in all particulars like a Lunatic Asylum proper.

*See Note I, p. 48.

4.   In a large proportion of cases insanity when taken in its early stages may be cured by proper treatment. True economy therefore, as well as humanity requires that provision for the Insane should be ample and well devised with a view to the relief of the public from the necessity of their support.

---

5.   It is universally acknowledged by experts that poor living is one of the main causes of insanity through physical deterioration, and that the best medicine for the insane is, in a large proportion of cases, nourishing food. The fact that the insane inmates of the Poorhouses are paupers should not then condemn them to paupers' fare. The following dietary is recommended by the State Commissioner in Lunacy.

STATE OF NEW YORK, OFFICE OF THE STATE COMMISSIONER IN LUNACY, ROSLYN, QUEENS CO.
November 27, 1876

Cheap Dietary for the Insane.

1)   *Fresh Meats and Fish, in preference to salted. The latter when kept in pickle lose all their albumillates, and become practically innutritious. They are not cheap at any price.*

2)   *Milk and Cheese. Both cheap in the country, and very nutritious. The richer in quality, the cheaper in their results as food.*

3) *Graham Flour, Oatmeal, Corn Meal, made in any form, and better without sweetening.*

4) *Potatoes, Beans, Peas, Carrots, Cabbage, Onions, Tomatoes, and Corn in their season, also Pumpkins.*

5) *Pickles occasionally. Vinegar should be daily on the table. Pickled Beets answer very well.*

6) *Apples, when they can be procured or apple sauce in winter and spring. No Pork (except to flavor with, or cook) or Buckwheat should be used.*

7) *Tea (weak) also Coffee to the aged and infirm in digestion and those long accustomed to it, but milk is better if it agrees, also Cocoa shells.*

This is as cheap a dietary as can be well drawn up in view of the end contemplated. Anything less than this should not be tolerated.

JOHN ORDRONAUX,
STATE COMMISSIONER IN LUNACY.

---

6.   Healthful occupation for the Insane is most desirable. Many will be found quite able to do such work as they have been in health accustomed to, and caution may be needed to guard them against over exertion. Gardening and out-of-door work of various kinds are especially recommended. Needle work, worsted-work and knitting may be provided for some. Others will with pleasure listen to reading or singing or be led to engage in simple games. Pictures hung upon the walls and a supply of books and illustrated papers will be found of service.

7.   The quarters occupied by the Insane should be well ventilated and well warmed, cheerful and light. Insane patients particularly need sunlight, and frequent moderate out of door exercise is very desirable for them.

---

8.   In order that insane patients may be taken out of doors at proper intervals and that the duty of caring for them may not become excessive, the number of attendants appointed for them should be larger than it usually is in Poorhouses. It must not be forgotten that this service requires much patience, gentleness and close attention, and that it is very wearing.*

*See Note 2, p. 48.

---

9.   Care should be taken that the Insane be kept clean and that the supply of warm clothing and bed·coverings for them be ample.

---

10. Owing to the insufficiency of accommodation for the chronic insane in the State Asylums, there are at present many such cases in the Poorhouses of counties not authorized by law to retain them. Although a few suggestions are given above with reference to their care, the State Charities Aid Association cannot too strongly protest against the sys tem of keeping any insane persons in Poorhouses. The State should make provision for all cases unless there are a sufficient number in any

county to warrant separate and suitable buildings for them, under the charge of physicians especially educated in the care of the Insane.*

*For further details upon this subject see Third Annual Report of the State Charities Aid Asso.; (Doc. No. 7), pages 20 and 21.

––––––––––––––

11. Children between the ages of seven and fourteen who are idiotic or so deficient in intelligence as to be incapable of being educated at any ordinary school, and who are not epileptic, or greatly deformed, may be admitted to the New York Asylum for Idiots at Syracuse.** Application should be made to the Superintendent. State pupils are received from all the counties, an equal number, as far as practicable, from each judicial district. All pupils are received upon trial for one month. State pupils are sup ported by the State, the charge for clothing being made to the counties of which the pupils are residents.

This Asylum is strictly an educational institution. To meet the needs of unteachable and adult cases of Idiocy another institution is needed.

For directions for care of unteachable idiotic children in Poorhouses see Letter on Care of Children-Appendix D.

**See Note 3, p. 48.

NOTES.

1. A second Asylum for the Chronic Insane was opened at Binghampton in October, 1881. The State is districted between the Binghampton and Willard Asylums, but the districts, as well as the counties exempted from the obligation to send their Insane to these Asylums, are liable to change. The State Charities Aid Association of the State Board of Charities will always furnish information in regard to the districts and the exempted counties.

2. In the well-managed pauper asylums of Scotland, the attendants number about one to every twelve patients. Lunatics need also a night-nurse.

3. A "Custodial Branch" for Female Idiots has been opened at Newark. See Appendix G, 5.

PART VII.

ABLE-BODIED PAUPERS.

1. The funds of the Poorhouse are obtained by a tax levied on the property of all citizens for the care of those who have no other means of support. No part of them can be willfully applied to other purposes except by misappropriation and a betrayal of trust.

Hence a searching examination of the ground of all applications for admission to the Poorhouse and especially for the admission of able-bodied paupers is essential to its honest management.

If the need for public support comes from persistent intemperance, improvidence or indolence, the applicant should be admitted only upon regular legal commitment as a vagrant, and should immediately, and as long as he is held in detention, be compelled to labor for his living.

Only in this way can the present rapid enlargement of this class be arrested.

---

2. As to methods of employment, every article used in the Poorhouse which can be made without machinery should be manufactured in it. There should be work enough on the farm to employ the able-bodied men during the greater part of the year, and indoor work should be laid out ahead for the winter months, for the rainy days and for those who cannot labor on the farm and in the garden.

The women should make all the clothing and bedding used and do the scrubbing and washing of the house. They should take part, under supervision, in the garden work. They should knit stockings, sew strips for rag carpeting, etc. A special workroom should be provided, in which they should be ordered to assemble at a fixed hour every day and be taught to cut and sew neatly, under a competent superintendent.

Whatever work is done by the able-bodied paupers should be done not at their option, but under a rigidly enforced system.

---

3. When it is found that an application from an able-bodied pauper for admittance to the Poorhouse has been the result purely or mainly of misfortune, the Committee should seek to make the stay of the sufferer in it as short as possible and to prevent his feeling an excessive sense of degradation.

If the aid of kindred cannot be obtained to relieve the necessity which holds him in the Poorhouse, it may be found that some not costly assistance, such as the supply of the tools of a trade, stolen or destroyed by a fire, or an introduction to an employer, will restore a man to independence.

In such cases caution may be needed to prevent the pauper from receiving the aid either as something to which he is entitled, on the one hand, or abjectly, as alms might be accepted by a beggar, on the other. The service should appear as closely as possible of the character of common neighborly kindness. If tools are furnished, for example, it is better that it should be in the form of a loan.*

*Sound advice on this difficult subject will be found in *Manual for the Visitors to the Poor*, by John W. Kramer, M.D. assistant minister of St. Mark's Church, New York City.

4. The Committee will do well to bear in mind that public opinion rightly assumes that when employment is asked for a man as a charity, there is a probability that he suffers more or less under some form of weakness or vice, and will not earn equal wages with those who have been able to look out for themselves.

Those for whom employment is obtained should not be made or allowed to feel that less or more than the usual measure of services can be expected in requital of the wages to be paid. The engagement should be a matter of business simply, not of favor or patronage, any more on the one side than on the other.

In dealing with men of doubtful character, it is always best, if possible, that payments should be arranged to be made not by the day or hour, but by the piece or job.

———————

5. The infamous custom of regarding public employment as a bounty, to be distributed under the name of patronage by the successful competitors for the offices controlling it, leads public works to be looked to by a large class as a form of charity alternative to that of the Poorhouse. This idea is most demoralizing and the habits of thought to which it gives rise are by far a greater and more costly evil than all those with which the Association is directly contending. The Committee is therefore advised to tolerate any wrong and let any suffering go unrelieved rather than give countenance to it.

PART VIII

CHILDREN.

1. In the year 1875 a law was enacted ordering the removal from, and forbidding the admission into, any Poorhouse of the State, of children of sound mind and body, over three years of age.*

This law was designed to end the very darkest chapter of all the gloomy history of our county charities, and that its importance may be realized and no specious arguments be accepted for temporizing with the evils against which it is directed, it can only be necessary that a fact should be known the statement of which the members of the Committee will probably be able to easily verify in their own experience. It is simply this, that of the present native pauper population of the State, of all ages, a large majority passed their earlier years in the Poorhouse and in it acquired their most deeply rooted ideas of life, society and social du ties. Educated in a community habitually dependent on charity, they have at a certain age; generally from fifteen to eighteen, been turned out with no strong or steadfast purpose of providing for themselves. Consequently as soon as they have met with any special discouragement or hardship they have naturally fallen back to the Poorhouse as a refuge, often bringing with them young children to repeat their degrading experience and again reproduce their kind.

*See Appendix C.

---

2. To get the better of this hereditary pauperism, and of innumerable evils which originate in it, and to give each generation a

chance to right itself, and rise to a higher plane, it is essential that the law should be strictly enforced, and on this point the Committee can, if occasion offers, take at once a resolute attitude. If the Superintendents are found to disregard the law in a single instance they should be made to understand that on a repetition of the offense they will subject themselves to indictment.

A special place outside the Poorhouse should be provided for occasions when it may be necessary to take care of a child for a few nights, for the detention of a child even for a single night in the Poorhouse is much to be deplored.

---

3.   On the other hand, the Committee will in no way do more beneficent work than in the aid it may give the Superintendents in finding kind, sensible and thrifty people to take charge of destitute children and in keeping an eye upon them in their new homes.

As early as possible, and in every case before any child in the Poorhouse is three years old, a decent home should have been sought out for it. The younger a child is when adopted, the more likely it is to become firmly endeared to its new guardians.*

*See Note 1, p.58.

---

4.   The action of the law of 1875 is limited to children of sound mind and body and excepts those who are "unteachably idiotic, epileptic, paralytic or otherwise defective or unfit for family care." When, therefore, the infirm in mind who are teachable shall have been sent to the Asylum at Syracuse, which is now being enlarged, and the

blind and deaf and dumb children to the appropriate State institutions, there will still remain in the Poorhouses a class for whom the State has not as yet made suitable provision. These unfortunates should have the Committee's most tender care.**

**See Note 2, p.58.

-----

5.   The rooms in which they live should be sunny and pleasant. The tables and chairs should be low, so that the children may see and reach with ease the objects placed before them.

-----

6.   In all fair weather, they should be kept a greater portion of the daytime out of doors.

They should not be turned over to 'the company of the old and gloomy, but as much as practicable given employment with the young and cheerful.

It is most desirable that occupations should be sought for them in which they can be useful. Out of doors this may be perhaps the picking of weeds, the gathering of loose stones or other matter which en cumber or litter the yards, roads and grounds; the sweeping of turf or of paved or flagged surfaces; the gathering of seeds, and the breaking and forming of brushwood into fagots for kindling or oven wood.

Indoors, sweeping, dusting, washing dishes, sewing, knitting, caring for and amusing younger children.

Simply to provide such children with toys and picture-books, and teach them how to amuse them selves, will give much happiness.*

*To feel more keenly how much it is possible to make of life to a class of children often left to mope almost in solitude, strangers to sympathy with active and healthy natures, it may be well for the visitor to recall the story of the "Little Mother" in "Little Devil."

---

7. All children in the Poorhouse should be kept scrupulously clean.

The greatest care should be taken that diseases of the skin, head, eyes, etc., be not communicated from one child to another by the use of the same towels, wash-cloths, handkerchiefs, combs or brushes.

Well children should not be allowed to remain with the sick.

Overcrowding is especially injurious to the young. They are much more quickly and seriously affected by foul air than grown people and most seriously at night.

The rooms in which they sleep should be thoroughly ventilated.

---

8. Their clothes should be large enough to allow free exercise of the limbs.

If they have trouble with the eyes, no bandages should be worn over them except by order of the physician. When young children are carried out to walk, their eyes should be protected from the direct rays of the sun.

9. It is not considered healthy for a young child to sleep in the same bed with an old person, but in Poorhouses old women may sometimes be found who will take better care of the children than the young.

In the Appendix a letter is given upon the "Diet and Care of Infants," written by a lady who has much experience and knowledge in the matter, and "Suggestions upon Feeding Babies" by a prominent physician of this city.*

*See Appendix D.

NOTES.

1. The law, as amended, forbids the retention of children in the Poorhouse after *two* years of age. It would be better still to remove them before they begin to talk.
2. The law, as amended, orders the removal from the Poorhouse of all children without exception. But there is not provision outside of the Poorhouse for the maintenance of unteachably idiotic, epileptic, paralytic or diseased children, except the Custodial Institution at Newark for Idiot Girls (Appendix G, 5) and as "Homes" will not take them and no family cares to adopt them, a number of them remain to the care of whom the suggestions made above are applicable; yet whenever it is practicable, they should be removed from the Poorhouse.

APPENDIX.

A.

NOTES ON DISINFECTION.

(Compiled from the Instructions of the New York Board of Health.)

Fresh air and pure water, constant ventilation and thorough cleansing are natural means of preventing and destroying the causes of infection and disease, but there may be infected places and things, and there are times of special necessity or sudden danger which require the instant arrest or destruction of the infection and all its removable causes: this is disinfection. The clothing from persons with small-pox, scarlatina or typhus, and even the air in the sick rooms of such patients, is infectious; and the sick with typhoid fever discharge excremental matters which possess infective properties that should be immediately destroyed.

There are several classes of disinfectants, each having specific uses. Some accomplish but one object; others two or more; some may be combined with advantage, others not.

COPPERAS AND CARBOLIC ACID.

Mix and stir briskly in five gallons of water, of dry copperas (sulphate of iron) eight pounds; of fluid carbolic acid half a pint.

The waste pipes of all water closets should be cleansed daily by flushing with water, after which half a pint of the above solution may be poured into each pan.

The same may be used to disinfect any waste pipes, sinks, drains or other foul places best reached by a liquid.

QUICKLIME.

To absorb moisture and putrid fluids, use fresh stone lime finely broken. Sprinkle it on the place to be dried, and in damp rooms place a number of plates or pans filled with the lime powder; whitewash with pure lime and not with kalsomine.

CHARCOAL POWDER.

To absorb the putrid gases, the coal must be dry and fresh and should be combined with lime. This powder is the calx powder as sold in the shops.

CHLORIDE OF LIME.

To give off chlorine, to destroy putrid effluvia, and to stop putrefaction, use it as lime is used, and if in cellars or close rooms the chlorine gas is wanted, pour strong vinegar or diluted sulphuric acid upon plates of chloride of lime occasionally and add more of the chloride.

TO DISINFECT ROOMS, ETC.

Where contagious diseases have occurred (including erysipelas, puerperal fever and repeated cases of diarrheal or dysenteric disorders) rooms and furniture should be disinfected by the following process:

Vacate the room for twelve hours; close every window and aperture, and upon an iron pipkin or kettle with legs, burn several ounces of sulphur. The quantity required for effectual work will depend upon the cubical space of the apartment, and there should be enough to burn rapidly until want of oxygen in the air shall extinguish the flame. Instantly after kind ling it, let every person withdraw from the place, and the room remain closed for the succeeding eight hours. Fumigation should be resorted to only under the personal superintendence of a competent medical man, as the disinfecting gases are poisonous.

To Disinfect Clothing.

Cast it into boiling water and let it remain with the water constantly boiling before washing.

Clothing from the sick should always be kept and washed apart.

Sunlight and Free Circulation of Air.

Let it never be lost sight of that these are the best agents of disinfection and that they can by the use of no expedients be dispensed with. Frequently open and let the air sweep through all cellars and places to which it cannot be constantly admitted. If damp and offensive surfaces are found within them apply fresh lime or calyx powder.

B.

LAW REGARDING THE SUPPORT OF RELATIVES

Code of Civil Procedure,
Title VIII, Sections 914-926.

Sec. 914. The father, mother, and children of sufficient ability, of a poor person who is insane, blind, old, lame, impotent, or decrepid, so as to be unable by work to maintain himself, must, at their own charge, relieve and maintain him in a manner to be approved by the Overseers of the town where he is, or in the city of New York, by the Commissioners of Charities and Correction.

Sec. 915. If a relative of a poor person fail to relieve and maintain him, as provided in the last section, the Overseers of the Poor of the town where he is, or in the city of New York, the Commissioners of Charities and Corrections, may apply to the Court of Sessions of the county where the relative dwells, for an order to compel such relief, upon at least ten days' written notice, served personally, or by leaving it at the last place of residence of the person to whom it is directed, in case of his absence, with a person of suitable age and discretion.

Sec. 916. At the time appointed in the notice, the Court must proceed summarily to hear the allegations and proofs of the parties, and must order such of the relatives of the poor person mentioned in section nine hundred and fourteen, as were served with the notice and are of sufficient ability to relieve and maintain him, specifying in the order the sum to be paid weekly for his support, and requiring it to be paid by the father, or if there be none, or if he be not of sufficient ability, then by the children, or if there be none, or if they be not of sufficient ability, then by the mother.

Sec. 917. If it appears that any such relative is unable wholly to maintain the poor person, but is able to contribute toward his support, the Court may direct two or more relatives, of different degrees, to maintain him, prescribing the proportion which each must contribute for that purpose; and if it appear that the relatives are not of sufficient ability wholly to maintain him, but are able to contribute something, the Court must direct the sum, in pro portion to their ability, which they shall pay weekly for that purpose.

Sec. 918. The order may specify the time during which the relatives must maintain the poor person, or during which any of the sums directed by the Court are to be paid, or it may be indefinite, or until the further order of the Court. The Court may from time to time vary the order, as circumstances may require, on the application either of any relative affected by it, or of an officer on whose application the order was made, upon ten days' written notice.

Sec. 919. The costs and expenses of the application must be ascertained by the Court, and paid by the relatives against whom the order is made; and the payment thereof, and obedience to the order of maintenance, and to any order for the payment of money, may be enforced by attachment.

Sec. 920. If a relative, required by an order of the Court to relieve or maintain a poor person, neglect to do so in the manner approved by the officers mentioned in section nine hundred and fourteen, and neglect to pay to them weekly the sum prescribed by the Court, the officers may maintain an action against the relative, and recover therein the sum prescribed by the Court, for every week the order has been disobeyed, to the time of the recovery, with costs, for the use of the poor. In the city of New York, the action must be in the name of the corporation of that city.

Sec. 921. When the father, or the mother being a widow or living separate from her husband, absconds from the children, or a husband from his wife, leaving any of them chargeable or likely to become chargeable upon the public, the officers mentioned in section nine hundred and fourteen may apply to any two Justices of the Peace or Police Justices in the county in which any real or personal property of the father, mother, or husband is situated, for a warrant to seize the same upon due proof of the facts, the magistrate must issue his warrant, authorizing the officers so applying to take and seize the property of the person so absconding.

Sec. 922. The officers so applying may seize and take the property, wherever it may be found in the same county; and are vested with all the right and title thereto, which the person absconding then had. The sale or transfer of any personal property, left in the county from which he absconded, made after the issuing of the warrant, whether in payment of an antecedent debt or for a new consideration, is absolutely void. The officers must immediately make an inventory of the property seized by them, and return it, together with their proceedings, to the next Court of Sessions of the county where they reside, there to be filed.

Sec. 923. The Court, upon inquiring into the circumstances of the case, may confirm or discharge the warrant and seizure; and if it be confirmed, must, from time to time, direct what part of the personal property must be sold, and how much of the proceeds of the sale, and of the rents and profits of the real property, if any, are to be applied towards the maintenance of the children or wife of the person absconding.

Sec. 924. If the party against whom the warrant issued return and support the wife or children so abandoned, or give security satisfactory to any two Justices of the Peace, or Police Justices in the city, village, or town, to the Overseers of the Poor of the town, or in the city of New York, to the Commissioners of Charities and Corrections, that the wife or children so abandoned shall not be chargeable to the town or county, then the warrant must be discharged by an order of the magistrates, and the property taken by virtue thereof restored to the party.

Sec. 925. The officers must sell at public auction the property ordered to be sold, and receive the rents and profits of the real property of the person absconding, and in those cities, villages or towns which are required to support their own poor, the officers charged therewith must apply the same to the support of the wife or children so abandoned; and for that purpose must draw on the County Treasurer, or in the city of New York, upon the Comptroller, for the proceeds as directed by special statutes. They must also account to the Court of Sessions of the county for all money so received by them, and for the application thereof, from time to time, and may be compelled by that Court to render that account at any time.

Sec. 926. In those counties where all the poor are a charge upon the county, the Superintendents of the Poor are vested with the same powers as are given by this title to the Overseers-of the Poor of a town in respect to compelling relatives to maintain poor persons, and in respect to the seizure of the property of a parent absconding and abandoning his family; and are entitled to the same remedies in their names, and must perform the duties required by this title, of Overseers, and are subject to the same obligations and control.

C.

CHILDREN'S LAW.

LAWS OF **1884,** CHAPTER **438.**

An act to revise and consolidate the statutes of the State relating to the custody and care of indigent and pauper children by orphan asylums and other charitable institutions. Passed May 31, 1884; three-fifths being present.

Sec. 2. It shall not be lawful for any County Superintendent or Overseer of the Poor, Board of Charity, or other officer to send any child between the ages of two and sixteen years, as a pauper, to any county poor-house or alms-house for support and care, or to detain any child between the ages of two and sixteen years in such poor-house or alms-house; but such County Superintendents, Overseers of the Poor, Boards of Charities, or other officers, shall provide for such child or children, in families, orphan asylums, hospitals, or other appropriate institutions, as provided by law. The Boards of Supervisors of the several counties of the State are hereby directed to take such action in the matter as may be necessary to carry out the provisions of this section. When any such child shall be so provided for or placed in any orphan asylum or such other institution, such child shall, when practicable, be so provided for or placed in such asylum or such other institution as shall then be controlled by persons of the same religious faith as the parents of such child.

D.

DIET AND CARE OF CHILDREN.

NURSERY AND CHILD'S HOSPITAL
Country Branch, West New Brighton, S.I., July 30.

DEAR * * *:

In order to understand how to improve the condition of poor children, we must first become familiar with the habits of their parents. The *causes* of diseases of skin, eyes and ears then become apparent. The ignorant believe that the more clothing a child has on, the better it is. If a clean suit is given, the mother will not remove the soiled clothes, but adds the new. This clothing with its numerous fastenings, is being constantly pushed up under the arms. The hands and feet become blue and cold from impeded circulation. Blankets are added when placed in bed; a perspiration follows. The discomfort produced by all this, makes the child cry. The child is taken up, blankets and coverings are hastily thrown off, and the perspiration is suddenly checked by contact with cooler air. This often lays the foundation of bronchitis and pneumonia. While suffering from these diseases of the respiratory organs and the help less infant is gasping for breath, the mother or nurse will place her heavy hand on the chest, adding to the difficulty of breathing.

Ignorant people cover the heads and even faces of their children, endangering suffocation, besides the unavoidable necessity of breathing the same air constantly. A thick covering close to the mouth and nose is not uncommon, and the heat of the head leads to sore heads, sore eyes, sore ears and boils. It must be understood that all this is from mistaken kindness, and the most tender mothers need watching, as well as careless nurses. Impress upon them the fact that there is more danger from too much heat, than from too great cold. Sore eyes are also caused by the exhalations from wet or damp floors. Constant scrubbing, instead of improving their condition, adds to the trouble. Exhalations from turpentine or soft soap, and the fibres of wood loosened by scrubbing, irritate the tender eyes. No child should stay in a room recently scrubbed. If a floor is covered with Linoleum (which is made of cork and warm}, it can be kept clean without danger to children. Unless a carpet can be constantly changed which would be troublesome, as well as expensive, it should not be used where there are several children. The habit of wrapping a child in the mother's shawl is almost universal. These shawls, already having absorbed moisture and bad odors from the mothers' bodies, are then impregnated with others from the secretions of children. The shawls are seldom or never washed, and they go on, increasing in unhealthfulness and to sore eyes and ears are added chafed skins and eruptions.

In an institution, a diaper should never be used a second time without washing. No turpentine soap should ever be used for washing either the bodies or clothing of infants. Borax soap for the clothing and borax and oatmeal soap for the persons will be found to be excellent.

Remove any soiled article immediately. The smell of the excretions can give disease, especially in summer, when cholera infantum is to be expected. It is all important to guard against damp clothing. Where there is a limited supply, it is unavoidable. It is much better to keep a *few* infants in good health, than a great many in only tolerable condition. The few will have stamina to become strong and useful members of society, while the many lead wretched lives, becoming paupers, and transmitting scrofula from generation to generation. Overcrowding leads to disease and death. With the kindest intentions benevolent women have sacrificed the lives of many children that might have been saved.

Avoid all patent medicines and soothing syrups. When a child cries, it may be either from tight clothing or indigestion. A warm flannel placed over the bowels, after a good rubbing, is generally much better than medicine. Avoid the *habit* of giving medicine for every trifling disturbance. A child soon learns to depend on it. Opiates are the resort of ignorant or indolent mothers or nurses.

FOOD. Nature should provide the proper nourishment for infants, but the unhealthy food and irregular lives, common among the poor, prevent mothers from giving what is needed, either in quantity or quality. It is too late now, to give the present race of mothers good health, or improve the almost extinct power of wet nursing. But it is left for those who study cause and effects, to stamp out scrofula, and improve the next generation, by doing all that is possible from the birth of children, and by attending more closely to ante-natal influences.

* * * * * Experience must determine in each case what is best. Only general rules can be given. While some thrive on cows' milk properly mixed with water, others improve on condensed milk. Barley water and milk is generally a safe and nourishing diet, or gluten carefully prepared, and mixed with milk. Milk in some form is necessary. At four or five months, a little bread or rolled cracker may be added. When the teeth appear, the diet must be strengthened. At two years, broth or soup can be given, varying the diet occasionally with oatmeal, rice or hominy. At three years, give meat once a day. A scrofulous child needs butter or fat. None but good butter should be given. A rind of salt pork, with a little fat left on and nicely broiled, is greedily enjoyed by scrofulous or delicate children.

When a child is unfortunate enough to have contracted the itch, the rule above mentioned about soap is laid aside. A good rubbing with ordinary soft soap is the first thing to be done, before employing the customary remedies. This will prevent the spread of disease. The ordinary kind can with care be cured in a few days. The other, which bears the common name of "seven years" or Army Itch, takes a month or six weeks, although occasionally it seems to be cured before, but it is liable to break out again, even after months elapse. Watch this well. It is always preventable in hospitals.

VENTILATION. It is impossible to lay too much stress on the necessity for watching the ventilation of every room both night and day. If not carefully inspected, at least once an hour, the windows and doors will be shut. In summer the transoms over the doors should be taken out, so as to make it impossible to prevent fresh air from outside being admitted into every room. Of course the halls must have fresh air constantly, and always supplied.

An open fire-place in every room is an important ventilator. In summer place a lamp in the grate, to draw all the bad air from the floor. It is necessary to bear in mind the fact that heated air ascends, foul · air descends. A ventilating flue of good dimensions should be in every room where there is an open fire place. An opening must be in the lowest part of this flue, so that the foul air near the floor shall escape. The fresh air coming in near the ceiling, through· transoms, will pass through the heated air at the up per part of the room, and will prevent a cold draught reaching the bed. Heating by radiation is better than furnace heat, but in very large rooms both are often needed. In summer a child should be kept in the open air as much as possible. Let every ward be emptied, and allow infants to eat and sleep outside. A room with several children is unbearable in the morning, unless the air is constantly changed.

It would be better to break out a pane of glass than to allow a window to be closed at the top. Sore eyes and cholera infantum may be expected if these rules for ventilation are neglected.

BATHING. Infants and children should be thoroughly bathed every morning, and if possible every evening as they sleep better after a bath. Great care should be taken to dry the body without rough rubbing. Ignorant mothers allow a black scurf to accumulate on the heads of infants, and refuse to remove it, for fear of "catching cold." No fine comb should be used on an infant's head. Sweet oil at night and borax soap in the morning will keep the head clean. If there is any appearance of soreness, tar soap can be used with advantage. The mouth· should be washed out every morning, and a little cold water swallowed once or twice in the day, especially in summer.

A powder of Lycopodeum will cure chafing, but with care it is seldom needed.

In case of ecsema, a little bran in the tepid bath is soothing, or·the flowers of the elderberry. These also stop the itching produced by mosquito bites.

These are a few of the rules required by those who visit among the poor, either in County Houses or families. If women can be taught the reason for adopting them, we may hope for improvement both in mind and body.

Yours truly,

MARY A. DUBOIS.

E.

AN ACT TO CONFER UPON THE "STATE CHARITIES AID ASSOCIATION" THE POWER TO VISIT, INSPECT, AND EXAMINE ANY OF THE COUNTY POORHOUSES AND TOWN POORHOUSES AND CITY ALMSHOUSES WITHIN THE STATE.

CHAPTER 323 LAWS OF 1881.

The People of the State of New York, represented in Senate and Assembly, do enact as follows:

Sec. 1. Any Justice of the Supreme Court of the judicial district, within whose boundaries any of the public charitable institutions of the State herein after referred to is located, is hereby authorized to grant, on written application of the Board of Managers of the ''State Charities Aid Association" (a corporation organized under chapter three hundred and nineteen of the laws of eighteen hundred and forty-eight and amendatory acts), through its president or other designated officer, to such persons as may be named in said application, orders for the purpose of enabling them or any of them to visit, inspect, or examine in behalf of said Association, in the county in which the visitors so appointed shall reside, any of the county Poorhouses, and town Poorhouses, and city Almshouses within the State., and located within such judicial district. Each of such orders shall specify the institution or institutions to be visited, inspected, and examined, and the names of the per sons by whom the visitation, inspection, and examination are to be made, and shall be in force for one year from the date on which it shall have been granted, unless sooner revoked.

Sec. 2. It shall be the duty of any and all persons, in charge of each and every Poorhouse or Almshouse embraced in the order specified in the first section of this Act, to admit any or all of the persons named in the said order of the Justice of the Supreme Court, into every part of such institution, and to render the said persons so named in said order every facility within their power to en able them to make in a thorough manner their visit, inspection, and examination, which are hereby declared to be for a public purpose, and to be made with a view to public benefit. Obedience to the order herein authorized shall be enforced in the same manner and with like effect as obedience is enforced to an order or mandate made by a Court of Record.

Sec. 3.· It shall be the duty of the said corporation to make an annual report to the State Board of Charities.

Sec. 4. This Act shall take effect immediately.

F.

DRAFT OF CONSTITUTION FOR THE USE OF LOCAL VISITING COMMITTEES.

CONSTITUTION.

ARTICLE I.

The name of this Association shall be the "Local Visiting Committee of the County Poorhouse, State of New York," and its objects shall be to visit regularly and systematically all the departments of the County Poorhouse, with a view to the mental, moral, and physical improvement of its pauper inmates, and to bring about such reforms as may be practicable.

ARTICLE II.

The Committee shall be composed of both men and women, and shall work under the control and by the direction of the State Charities Aid Association, of which it forms part. No membership fee shall be required.

ARTICLE III.

The Officers of the Association shall be a President and Secretary. They shall be elected for the year by a two-thirds vote at the Annual Meeting. In case of the death or resignation of any officer, a successor for the remainder of the year may be elected by a two-thirds vote of members present at any regular monthly meeting of the Committee, one week's notice of such intention having been previously given to all members by the Secretary.

ARTICLE IV.

The President shall preside at all meetings of the Committee; shall call Special Meetings at discretion, or upon the written request of three members; and shall have the objects and general interests of the Committee in charge. The President shall appoint Special Committees, and in case of personal sickness or absence may appoint a Vice-President from among the members of the Committee.

ARTICLE V.

The Secretary shall keep minutes of· the proceedings of all the meetings of the Committee and of the meetings of the Executive Committee, and shall give notice of all Special Meetings. The Secretary shall report to the Secretary of the State Charities Aid Association as follows: a Monthly Report, as soon as practicable after the regular

Monthly Meetings of the Committee, and an Annual Report of the year's work and general condition of the affairs of the Committee, before the first of November.

ARTICLE VI.

There shall be an Executive Committee, composed of the officers of the County Committee, and three other members chosen for their sound judgment and general interest in the work of the Committee. The President of the Committee shall be the Chairman of this Executive Committee. It shall hold meetings on the same day and just before the regular Monthly Meeting of the County Committee, and oftener if desirable. It shall be the duty of the Executive Committee to devise ways and means for increasing the usefulness and efficiency of the County Committee. It shall prepare such regulations as may best promote the objects of the Association, and, when adopted by the Committee, shall have power to enforce them. It shall also be responsible for the observance, by all members, of the Articles of the Constitution. This Executive Committee shall put itself into communication with the Superintendents of the Poor and with the Keeper of the Poorhouse, and shall be the medium of intercourse between the Association and the Poor house officials. Complaints of any abuses existing in the Poorhouse, and suggestions for remedying them shall not be made directly by the Visitors to the Superintendents of the Poor, nor to the Keeper of the Poorhouse, nor to his wife, except by permission of the President of the Association. All such complaints and suggestions shall be brought before the Executive Committee at its next meeting, or, if requiring immediate attention, shall be reported to the President, who shall act upon them according to his or her best judgment.

ARTICLE VII.

The inmates of Poorhouses being divisible into three general classes-Children, Persons feeble or diseased in body or mind, and adult able-bodied Paupers,-it shall be the duty of this Association to direct its attention to each class, with the view of securing to each its proper care and treatment. It shall especially endeavor to; see that the law removing children from Poorhouses is rigidly enforced in the case of healthy children, and as far as practicable in the case of diseased children. Each visitor shall keep a note-book in which shall be entered an account of each visit, and any suggestions that may present themselves. Visitors' books shall be open, on application, to the perusal of any member of the Executive Committee.

ARTICLE VIII.

Advisory members may be added at the discretion of the Committee. Their duties shall be to further the objects of the Association by advice and active assistance, whenever called upon by the Executive Committee.

ARTICLE IX.

No spirituous liquors, provisions, or medicines of any kind shall be given to the paupers, except by permission of the Physician in charge, or of the Keeper of the Poorhouse, or his wife.

ARTICLE X.

Members shall constitute a quorum at any meeting of the Association. New members may be admitted by a two-thirds vote of members present at any regular meeting, the name of the proposed member having been sent in to the President three days before.

ARTICLE XI.

The Monthly Meetings of the Committee shall be held on of each month. The Annual Meeting shall be held

ARTICLE XII.

This Constitution may be amended by a two thirds vote of members present at any regular meeting of the Committee, two weeks' notice of such intention, with the text of the proposed amendment, having been previously given by the Secretary.

BY-LAWS.

NO. 1. Order of Business.

The following shall be the order of business at the regular meetings of the Committee.

1. The Secretary shall read the minutes of the last preceding meeting. Action thereon.
2. Report of Executive Committee. Action thereon.
3. Reports of Visitors. Action thereon.
4. Reports of Special Committees, if any, and action thereon.
5. The President shall read any written or printed communications from the State Charities Aid Association, or any other matter bearing upon the work of the Association.
6. New business.

There shall be no talking during the meetings, except by members addressing the Chair.

NO. II.

At any Special Meeting of the Committee, the business for which the meeting has been called shall be transacted, and no other.

In this Constitution there is no reference to the subject of Out-door relief, because the County Committees of the State Charities Aid Association are formed primarily for Poorhouse visitation. Attention to the means of keeping people out of the Poorhouses grows naturally out of this visitation, however, and some of the County Committees have consequently added to their original work a department of out-door relief. The Central Association, aware of the importance and the difficulty of so giving relief as not to pauperize the recipients, has as signed this subject, as one demanding special study, to a Standing Committee, called "The Committee on the Elevation of the Poor in their Homes," a name chosen because of its suggestiveness of the direction which out-door relief should take. The Association has adopted the following Article for the government of this Committee, and commends it to all "Local Visiting Committees" proposing to take up this department of work:

"It shall be the duty of the Committee on the Elevation of the Poor in their Homes: 1st. To try and secure co-operation between officials and volunteers in the administration of out-door relief, and to bring about such reforms in the present system as may conduce to the reduction of pauperism. 2nd. To try and secure co-operation between organized charities, whether represented by churches, societies, or official out-door relief. 3rd. To advocate those practical measures in behalf of the poor which best promote self-support and self-respect, and which, in exceptional seasons of distress, shall so assist the worthy poor that they may be saved from becoming paupers."

G

ADDITIONAL SUGGESTIONS AND INFORMATION FOR VISITING COMMITTEES.

1. Local Visiting Committees should consist of both men and women, selected without reference to political party or religious denomination.

They should represent, as far as practicable, the unofficial, tax-paying public, and no person officially connected with the care of the poor should be a member of the Committee.

2. A Constitution and By-laws have been pre pared by the Association for the use of Local Visiting Committees (Appendix F), and may be adopted as drafted, or modified to suit local conditions. In every case it seems necessary to the efficiency of a Committee that it should adopt a Constitution defining its duties and regulating its action.

A certain number of the members of each Local Committee will be nominated for legal appointment as Visitors (see Appendix E); the pro portion of such appointments to the whole number of the Committee being determined by the President of the Central Association.

3. Under the Poor-Laws of New York executive authority in all matters relating to paupers is vested in the Superintendents of the Poor; they are the .proper officers to whom to apply for the remedy of abuses. The function of the Supervisors is, in the main, legislative

Great care should be taken to avoid unauthorized individual interference with the administration of the County Institutions. By the terms of the Constitution recommended to the Local Commit tees, Visitors are forbidden to make complaint or adverse criticism to the officials or at the Poor house. Courteous suggestion or, it may be, explicit protest on the part of the committee as a whole, *t/zrQUg/z* its President, may be required. But it should be clearly understood that public exposure of errors in the management of county institutions should be resorted to only when all else has failed ·to effect reform.

———————————

4.   Frequent correspondence between the Central Association and its Local Committees is of vital importance to both. From the sum of the reports it receives the Association frames measures of general reform; while Committees just entering upon the work are enabled by such correspondence to benefit by the experience of those of longer standing.

Each Local Committee should send in its re ports at stated times-monthly, quarterly, or semi annually. If there is nothing to report, it should report that fact. The reports should be written in official form, should be as concise as is consistent with fullness, and, for convenience of filing, should be written upon paper of uniform size, preferably foolscap.

Whatever extra-official communication the Secretary of the reporting Committee may have to make should accompany the report as a separate letter.

5.   The Custodial Branch of the Idiot Asylum, at Newark, is intended to receive the adult idiotic and feeble-minded females from the various Poorhouses and Almshouses of the State.

For adult idiotic and epileptic males a similar institution is greatly needed. In the Poorhouses they lead a miserable life, and they cause a great deal of trouble and annoyance.

SUGGESTIONS UPON FEEDING BABIES.

Taken from "Infant Diet" by A. Jacobi, M.D., Professor of Diseases of Children, College of Physicians and Surgeons, New York.

Boil a teaspoonful of powdered barley, (ground in a coffee mill kept for the purpose,) and a gill of water, with a little salt, for fifteen minutes, strain it and mix with half as much boiled milk and a lump of white sugar. Give it lukewarm with a nursing bottle. Keep both bottle and mouth-piece in a bowl of water when not in use.

For babies of five or six months half barley water and half boiled milk, with salt and white sugar.

For still older babies, more milk in proportion. When babies are very costive, use oatmeal instead of barley. Cook and strain.

When breast milk is half enough, change off between breast milk and food.

In hot summer weather, try the food with a small strip of blue litmus paper. If the blue paper turns red, either make a fresh mess, or add a small pinch of baking soda to the food.

Infants of six months may have beef-tea or beef soup once a day, by itself or mixed with the other food.

Babies of ten or twelve months may have a crust of bread and a piece of rare beef to suck.

Give no candies.

Chapter 3

He's Only a Pauper, Whom Nobody Owns! (1910)

I t seems very fitting that James Oppenheim choose the 1841 words of Thomas Noel from his poem, "The Pauper's Drive," as the title for his early 20th century exposé on the shocking conditions prevalent in many poorhouses in our nation. Noel's verse very poignantly describes the last "road trip" of many individuals who lived and died in our country's institutions of custodial care.

There's a grim one-horse hearse in a jolly round trot--
To the churchyard a pauper is going, I wot;
The road it is rough, and the hearse has no springs;
And hark to the dirge which the mad driver sings;
Rattle his bones over the stones!
He's only a pauper whom nobody owns!

In his "American Magazine" article, Oppenheim well describes the gravity of the situation prevalent in late 19th century poorhouses. In defining an almshouse, he notes one would by nature suppose it to be the last refuge for the old men and women who are too weak to work, alone, homeless, friendless and penniless, having crept there to die. But alas, these poor souls are not alone there. The senior citizens, whose only crime is old age and misfortune, are crowded and herded in like cattle with other displaced souls: the blind, intemperate, sick, cripple, feeble-minded, vagrant, lame and pregnant. As Oppenheim suggests, this cocktail of unfortunates, to an outside observer, is inhumane, indecent and intolerable. To his credit, Oppenheim ends his treatise with five very good suggestions to make improvements to the conditions prevalent in that era.

"He's Only a Pauper, Whom Nobody Owns!"

BY

JAMES OPPENHEIM

AUTHOR OF "DR. RAST," ETC.

ILLUSTRATED WITH PHOTOGRAPHS BY BROWN BROS. AND F. B. CATTON

THIS is a revolting article, but it must be printed. The things described are almost unbelievable. You must go back to the old Bedlam to find anything so revolting in the case of suffering human beings.

A citizen of Missouri, reading the article, may feel inclined to rise in wrath against New York State. A Pennsylvania man might be prompted to throw stones over the border. The curious fact is, however, that the social experts believe New York to be in advance of most other States in its almshouse system. Then let the other States look to their own! Is it still true, as reported in 1904, that in Missouri almshouses and their inmates are farmed out to the lowest bidder? Is it true that, in one State a superintendent uses a horse-whip to quiet the insane? That an insane woman has been kept strapped to a bed six years? That in another State an insane man has been kept in a stockade, open to the sky, winter and summer, with hardly a shred of clothing on him for eleven years? Is it still true that such conditions exist throughout the South? That in Pennsylvania not only the feeble-minded, but the insane also, are herded in with rational human beings? Let the States look to their own!

It should be noted, by the way, that since this article was written the almshouse at Hempstead, L. I., has burned to the ground, with two missing and half a dozen injured. Most of the houses in New York State—crowded with human beings—would burn as quickly and as easily. It is pleasant to record that at Hempstead the superintendent and his wife plunged into the smoke and flames and helped bear out the sick and feeble. The photographs, taken a few days before the fire, have now a curious and tragic interest. THE EDITOR.

I T is easy to say that conditions in the almshouses of the State of New York are horrible. But it is all a matter of viewpoint. It is all a matter of how human beings should treat each other. For the inmates in almshouses have been selected from among us—they are men and women, mostly old—they have the needs, the desires, the frailties that we have. How shall we deal with them?

I asked the old Civil War veteran who is Superintendent of the Oneida County Almshouse in Rome, N. Y.:

"How can you stand it in this place?"

He said:

"Well, the first three months I was here I thought I'd go crazy. I told my wife I'd rather be dead than here. But I got used to it. It's like everything else. Live with it long enough, and you take it for granted."

Each county in New York State, with a few exceptions, has its own house for paupers; a local Board of Supervisors controls it; the State Board of Charities inspects it. Evidently all these officials have gotten "used to it," and "take it for granted." An outsider, however, seeing it for the first time, is apt to use violent language. For instance, this extract from a report on the Oneida County Almshouse, made December 1, 1907, by a well-known investigator:

"If I were to describe my conception of the horrors of Hades, I do not believe it could be more terrible than what I saw there. There is no attempt at classification or segregation of these poor unfortunate wretches. Many of

214

them should be in regular hospitals, some should be in insane asylums, and others, doubtless, should be in prison; but they mingle at will. No restraint is placed upon them. If perchance they come into possession of a dollar, they are at liberty to cross the street to Burke's Saloon, where they 'tank up' to the limit of their capacity. Ordinarily, this should be condemned; but under the circumstances I should say it is a great boon to anyone there who has the privilege of such an opportunity. These wretches, drunk or sober, may wander about the city at liberty.

"When it is too cold for them to be out, as it evidently was yesterday, they sit around in vile stuffy rooms without the slightest semblance of ventilation. The air was positively nauseating. This is not exaggeration. Several times I started for the door, thinking I was going to throw up my breakfast. They smoke their villainous pipes and spit wherever they choose. The institution is evidently taxed to its capacity. I was taken up into a dark, dirty attic, which was almost filled with filthy beds. I cannot imagine tenement-house conditions which could be much worse, and if I had the power to describe the so-called hospital ward, it would positively turn your stomach. There are no toilet facilities. The floors about the beds are actually spotted and in some places coated with refuse; not a window open, and the stench was sickening."

What is an almshouse? One would naturally suppose it to be the last refuge of the old—men and women too weak to work, alone in the world, homeless, friendless, penniless. One would expect to find the almshouse full of gentle old people, near death. Such people are in the almshouse. They have crept there to die. There they wind up their obscure lives, their humble destinies. These are the lonely and lowly tragedies of our packed world. But they are not alone with one another. I jotted down the following list from the Oneida County Almshouse register:

Old
Blind
Feeble-minded
Intemperate
Sick
Cripple
Epileptic
Vagrant
Lame
Pregnant

They are mixed in with one another. The decent old, whose only crime is old age and misfortune, are herded in with unspeakable creatures. Imagine sleeping in a dormitory with babbling idiots, with jerky epileptics, with hardened, vicious criminals, and with consumptives. Imagine spending the day and eating one's meals with this strange company. Such conditions, to an outsider, are inhuman, indecent and intolerable.

Let me describe one of these pest-houses—of which there are some twenty or thirty in New York State. The Oneida County Almshouse is situated out in the open country near Rome, N. Y. It is a large triple building, the center for the Superintendent and his family and helpers, the left wing for men, the right for women. It contains 246 men, 87 women. This is the usual proportion, 3 males to 1 female. And yet, stupidly enough, the women's side is an exact duplicate of the men's. The building, as almost all other such in the State, was put up without good judgment. The result is that the women have more room than they need, and the men are so crowded that the attic is used as a dormitory. This attic has ceilings sloping to the floor and but a few small windows. There is bad ventilation and poor light. Yet ninety cots are in this place, side by side, head to head, foot to foot. Ninety men of all types—the clean and the filthy, the sick and the feeble-minded, the blind and the halt—sleep here every night. There are some things relating to cleanliness and sanitation that cannot be put down in print, but one can imagine the indecency and foulness.

There is no privacy for a decent man. He keeps his hat on all day because his head is the only safe place for keeping it. The hat will disappear if left on his bed. This accounts for the fact that each man possesses only what is on his back. There is no change of clothes. Some of the men, human enough to want to have their little private property, stow it between the covers of the bed. The ex-city-editor of the Utica *Press* was an inmate because of intemperance. When he died his bed was found full of newspaper clippings. The bed of another man, when searched, revealed a tin can with the bait of worms crawling over the sheet. It is hard, of course, to keep these cots free of vermin, bedbugs and lice. It is hard to get 246 men to bathe regularly in the one tub at their disposal; and still harder to get them to use the showers. Many of them smell vilely.

When the cold days of autumn come the vagrants and tramps, looking for shelter, allow themselves to be arrested. They are committed to the almshouse. The burden of life is taken from their shoulders. They get a warm bed, warm housing, poorly prepared food that will sustain life, and a paper of tobacco. They spend the day in the large living room, playing cards, smoking, chewing, spitting, talking. Then, at times, they go forth on the highway, beg money from passersby and get drunk. They come back, quarrel and brawl with the other inmates, and cover the floors and beds with filth. It is against the law to sell liquor to an almshouse inmate, but the law is not enforced. Then, when the warm days of spring return, and the Superintendent is ready to call out all able-bodied inmates to work on the farm, the vagrants and tramps disappear. The number in winter runs up to 365. In summer it dwindles to about 150. Why are not these two hundred vagrants in jail or at work?

It is a great misfortune to be sick in the almshouse. Yet a doctor who investigated the Oneida County house, and who is now practising in New York, estimates that between 60 and 75 per cent. of the inmates are in need of medical or surgical attention. Out of this number a few are so downright ill that they are given separate rooms. One woman has consumption, with but a few weeks more to live. Another, formerly a trained nurse, is slowly dying of locomotor ataxia, and is a morphine fiend. Such people ought to have the best hospital care. Yet for all the almshouse there is only one visiting physician. He receives $400 a year, and the job is political. He comes every other day. *And there is not even one trained nurse.* There is a "practical nurse," a woman who has tended the sick for many years, and a couple of assistants. The inmates are left to care for each other. The blind man nurses the lame, the epileptic tends to the infirm.

Yet, connected by a passageway with the institution, stands a brand-new hospital. It is not being used, and for good reasons. About two years ago, after years of pressure from outsiders, the 49 supervisors of Oneida County elected a Committee of Five to report on building a hospital.

This Committee advised a building costing about $80,000, and then without waiting for further authority proceeded to build. They spent over $200,000. Instead of a hospital for 50, it is a hospital for 200. The supervisors have refused to pay the bills and the District Attorney is investigating. One of the Committee, Swancott, was mixed up in other graft in Utica and has been sentenced to jail for from 3 to 5 years on a charge of grand larceny. However, the doctor quoted above believes that if the hospital is used by the county, it will be a good investment. He fears, though, that it will not be used right, and has no confidence in the management. As an almshouse hospital, it is a gross absurdity, being nearly as large as the almshouse itself.

In the meantime, several hundred human beings are in the hands of a physician of whom the State Inspectors made the following report, January, 1908:

"It does not appear that this physician gives any attention to the sanitary condition of the rooms, nor to the segregation of patients afflicted with tuberculosis or erysipelas from other inmates. Apparently he gives no direction as to needed improvements in the general care of the sick, except to prescribe remedies for the particular cases called to his attention. He permits the attendant to distribute morphine without prescription to habitual users of the drug, a month's supply at a time, in quarter and eighth grain doses, a few of which if misplaced and taken by one not accustomed to its use would cause death, etc. . . . He says he has no equipment for determining whether a suspected case is tubercular or not. . . . The inmates have more confidence in their attendants than they have in him, and some of them say, 'The doctor doesn't believe in doctoring old, worn-out people. He says they don't need medicine. It will get their stomachs out of order.' 'Yes, he came to see me once when I was sick, but if it hadn't been for the nurse I guess I wouldn't be here now.' . . . It appears that many of the inmates use proprietary medicines at their own discretion. The officers of the almshouse, however, express great confidence in the physician's ability, but, while he may be conscientious, he is without the broad humanity, knowledge and energy necessary to bring up the medical care of the almshouse to the point of real efficiency."

Many of the almshouses have not even the promise of a hospital. Last October Commissioner Joseph C. Baldwin, Jr., of the State Board of Charities, investigated conditions at the Dutchess County almshouse. Out of the 100 inmates, there were 42 deaths in 14 months. He writes:

"On the day I visited the almshouse there were four inmates in what seemed a helpless and hopeless condition lying on their beds, receiving only such casual attention as could be rendered by the keeper and his wife at times when they were not busy with their other multitudinous duties.

"The Superintendent, though living on the grounds, rarely visits or gives any attention to the institution. The position of County Superintendent of the Poor, at least in Dutchess County, is regarded as a political plum, and the wretched inmates, should they fall ill, are left in a most pitiable state of neglect. The record of deaths as shown by our inspector's report is appalling, and it is my opinion that an

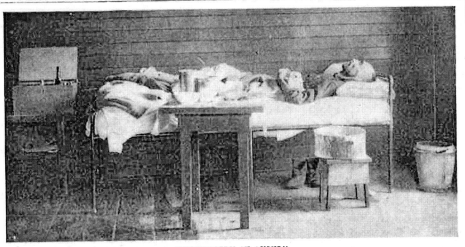

THE TRAGEDY AT AUBURN

nvestigation should be at once instigated, ither by the committee on almshouses of this oard or by the District Attorney of the county. "That the Board of Supervisors of Dutchess ounty should give so little attention to their ounty almshouse is to me inexplicable and alls for the severest condemnation."

It seems unbelievable, but in the Oneida County Almshouse 4 men have died of cancer. The last one sat in the crowded living room the past year, the whole side of his face eaten away, a horrible spectacle. His cheek, chin, nose and eye were half gone, and the smell of decaying flesh filled the room.

But most amazing of all is the experience of John A. Kingsbury, who is heading the State campaign against tuberculosis. In May, 1898, he visited the Cayuga County Almshouse in company with Dr. H. D. Pease, Director of the State Hygienic Laboratory, and C. W. Fetherol. The following is from the Auburn Citizen of Monday, May 18, 1908:

"Mr. Kingsbury showed Superintendent Andrew Trimble his credentials and asked to see those inmates who happened to be suffering from tuberculosis.

"Mr. Trimble stated that so far as he knew there was only one of these unfortunates, and he showed the party a small hut one hundred yards away from the main building, where the consumptive patient was located. They went down to the place and found a man of forty-two years dying of consumption. According to Mr. Kingsbury, he lay on a cot alone. Near him stood an ash barrel with ashes, into which he was supposed to expectorate, the ashes being subsequently buried. . . . The man said

he was forty-two years of age and had been ill since January. His voice was feeble and he was in a wretched physical state. Noticing a large quantity of sputum on the floor near the cot, Mr. Kingsbury remarked to the man: 'My good man, don't you know it is very unsanitary to spit on the floor like that? Why don't you use this ash can?'

"The patient nodded affirmatively that he knew he should spit into the can, but he said he was not strong enough to raise himself sufficiently to reach the can. Had he had proper treatment he would have been supplied with gauze cloths. While the visitors were looking over the place, the unfortunate man had a coughing spell and, somewhat ashamed of his previous though innocent disregard of sanitary rules, gathered together every ounce of his strength, raised himself on his cot, and with great effort managed to spit into the ash can. Then he dropped back on his cot with a heavy sigh and lay exhausted. He had not been shaved apparently in several weeks, and this fact, together with the emaciated condition of his body . . . made a picture of wretchedness impossible to conceive in our twentieth-century civilization.

"The man told the visitors that he had been a hard-working man until consumption had taken hold of him. The visitors returned to the main building, where they learned that one of the inmates had been detailed to act as nurse of the consumptive, but that he refused to remain in constant attendance because, 'It was too cold there.'

"Returning to Auburn, the trio decided that such awful conditions deserved to be exposed

to the citizens of this county, and they therefore made arrangements with Photographer
Catton to visit the place and to obtain photographs of the conditions. . . .

"Yesterday morning, the trio, accompanied
by Photographer Catton, went out to the institution. On arriving there they asked about
the condition of the consumptive.

"'Oh, I guess he is still alive,' said the Superintendent, and the party went to the little isolated place to see the man. Mr. Kingsbury
went in advance and called the man's name.
As the man did not answer, Mr. Kingsbury
touched him. *The man was dead.*"

The photograph is published herewith and
speaks for itself.

At Hempstead, L. I., where there are 50 inmates, of whom 6 are women, I found half a
dozen consumptives living right in with the
others. One miserable old fellow was sitting
alone in the cellar before the furnace, trying to
keep warm. I was told that recently a consumptive was committed to the house so far
gone that he died two days later. No reason
was given why a man so utterly sick was housed
with vagrants, idiots and the old, instead of
going to a hospital.

At Eastview, Westchester County, there are
two hospitals—one for consumptives. And
yet even here there is strange mismanagement.
The visiting physician, a Dr. Russell, comes but
seldom to the hospital. The actual work is in
the hands of two young men who have just
graduated from the medical college. The best
physicians of Westchester County have offered
their services free of charge. *Their offer has
been refused.* Recently an inspection committee found a woman with a hurt hip who
had been in the house a whole year without
treatment. The doctors knew nothing of the
case.

The Westchester buildings, too, are note-
worthy. The old main building from time to
time has had a wing added to it, each wing of
a different type, and so inadequate that every
inch of hall-space is taken up by cots. The
only meeting room for the men is in a cellar,
with tiny prison-windows. Here 150 men con-
gregate, so closely packed that in order to play
cards they have to use wooden horses instead
of tables, and the overflow sits about in the
dampness and foul smell of the adjoining wash-
room. A pretense is made here of setting able-
bodied men to work. I saw some twenty of
them breaking stones, chewing, spitting, chat-
ting, and now and then gently hitting a bit of
rock. However, at Westchester, new buildings are in course of construction—large dormitories, cheerless, unhomelike, where all the

errors of wholesale charity are being repeated.
And, although the almshouse population has
actually decreased in the last 30 years, the new
buildings have space for 700 people. The
present number at Westchester is about 400.

But examples could be multiplied indefi-
nitely. For instance, the house at Lockport,
Niagara County, an old stone building with 110
inmates. Kerosene lamps are still used there,
89 of them—a constant source of danger in the
hands of the old. The entire interior is rotting
away, and there are actually holes in the floor,
the cause—according to the keeper—of a small
fire in 1908. The halls and ceilings are old
and crumbling; the stairs are narrow and steep;
there are no bathing facilities for the women,
who are forced to use pails. I quote from the
State Inspector's report:

"Water is hauled to the almshouse in barrels
in the dry season and is used so sparingly that
it is insufficient to flush the drain pipes, so that
for several months the sewerage remains decaying in the pipes and forming deadly gases
which are ready to work back into the house
through any imperfect traps in the plumbing."

Among those in the almshouse are:

5 blind
2 deaf mutes
9 feeble-minded
2 epileptics
1 insane

There is a frame building used as a hospital.
It contains 31 patients. The report is as
follows:

"There is an operating table and some in-
struments, but no sterilizer. There are five
septic and contagious cases, two cancer patients, one syphilitic, one patient with tubercular sores, and one case with running abdom-
inal sores, the stench of which is fearful. A
pavilion for the isolation of such cases is a
necessity."

Possibly it may now be understood what an
almshouse is. It is the last refuge of the old;
it is the winter hotel of the vagrant; it is the
pest-house for the sick; the asylum for the
feeble-minded—it is, in short, the county's con-
venient dumping ground. Here the Charities
Commissioner, the Overseer of the Poor and
the magistrate commit the dependent, the defective and the delinquent. They are all
cooped up together and allowed to work out
their own destinies. One finds in the woman's
living room a spectacle of horror and poignant
sadness. Here is a woman of ninety, like a
child of three, doubled up in a little rocking
chair, singing wildly. Another woman sits by
whose nose is half eaten away by syphilis.
Next to her sits a degenerate who escapes from

THE MIDDAY MEAL: A BOWL OF THIN TEA, SOME BEEF-STEW, AND BREAD

the institution for a carouse whenever she can. Another, three feet high, in a wheel-chair, twitches and jerks with chorea. Another rocks to and fro, babbling incoherent fragments. Another has an ulcer wrapped in dirty bandages. And yet among such people some quiet old woman who is patiently waiting for death must spend her days. At night she sleeps in the common dormitory with these deformed or degenerate human beings.

The almshouses of New York are bad enough, but New York is considered the best State in this respect. An investigation in Missouri in 1904 disclosed the fact that the insane were housed in sheds without heat or light, and in Pennsylvania and New Jersey there is even a worse mixing in of the criminal and the sick with the innocent and the well.

Who is responsible? This is an age that prides itself on its social work. We have wonderful hospitals, we have new methods of dealing with criminals, we have model reformatories, tenement-house reform, civic movements, tuberculosis campaigns. Who, in the face of our new science and our new social ideals, is responsible for the almshouses?

The man directly in charge is the keeper. The job is political, the man elected. It is quite natural that his main qualification for office should be his "pull" rather than his character and training. The keeper at Oneida is an ex-Civil War veteran, kindly and ignorant;

at Westchester, the ex-keeper of Sing Sing prison; at Hempstead, the *ex-keeper of the cemetery*. As a rule the man is a farmer. Now, it is good to know that these keepers are usually simple and kindly men; but where kindliness is linked with inexperience and ignorance the results can hardly be good. In addition, these keepers will tell you that they have not enough help. They are kept busy merely keeping the place up, and cannot inaugurate improvements.

These keepers are under the direct control of the County Board of Supervisors. This Board raises and spends the money, inspects and governs the house. But as these men are usually local farmers, they too are without training or experience.

They, in turn, are subject to the inspection and criticism of the State Board of Charities. This Board could get a court order to compel county authorities to change conditions, but while they are severe enough in their criticisms and searching in their inspections, conditions go on with but slight modification.

What is needed is a vital change in the system.

First, put the almshouses in charge of the State. Centralize the control and the responsibility. Our State Institutions are all modern. —the buildings are fitted to their purpose, the Superintendents are trained — and are run on economic, human and scientific principles.

AN INMATE OF ALMSHOUSE AT HEMPSTEAD,
LONG ISLAND

It is estimated that the insane receive fifty times the amount and quality of care given to the almshouse inmates, and this at a less per capita expense. Under the State, the best experts could be secured and could be held responsible.

Second, drain the almshouses of all inmates not properly there. Put vagrants in jail, idiots in asylums for the feeble-minded, the sick in hospitals. If this were done, instead of 50 houses in the State, a dozen would be sufficient. This would mean economy and a concentration of enlightened effort.

Third, make the position of keeper a civil service job. Put in charge a trained man. For instance, the Woman's Reformatory at Bedford, Westchester County, is in charge of Miss Davis, a doctor of philosophy and an expert on dietetics. She has with her a resident woman physician and a staff of teachers. Or the Girls' Reformatory at Hudson, in charge of Dr. Hortense B. Bruce, a physician. Under such enlightened supervision, there is apt to be good housing, good food, good clothing, good care.

Fourth, do some constructive work with the inmates to make their lives worth while. This experiment has already been tried with great success by the Committee on Employment of Infirm of the State Charities Aid Association of New York.

It was begun in 1893 at the City Hospital

under Miss Rosalie Butler and has since been greatly extended. I quote a part of their very interesting report:

"It is particularly to the more helpless class of crippled, infirm, and blind inmates that we send a teacher who goes several times a week to the City Homes on Blackwell's Island and at Flatbush and to the City Hospital. The teacher begins her friendship with the inmates by learning their tastes and wishes in the line of work, and then gives them some suitable employment which will interest them, if necessary advancing them the materials required, for which they pay from the proceeds of the sale of the articles that they make. The aim of the teacher is to show the workers how to make articles of attractive design and of practical usefulness and the results obtained by many are excellent. They make baskets and mats of raffia and other materials, attractive beadwork chains, illuminated cards, shawls, aprons, rugs, hammocks, belts, screens and many other useful and ornamental articles.

"The work that they have completed we sell for their benefit. The small sums of money that they earn usually go to buy little articles of comfort, food, or clothing, which often are generously given away to their more helpless companions. Sometimes their money

A FEEBLE-MINDED NEGRO

s saved toward entering some private Home, r to help a relative in trouble.

"They appreciate greatly their chance to vork and earn a little money, always pitifully ittle. Many of them write us most grateful etters, and they all have a far more cheerful view of life and a friendlier spirit of comrade-hip than they had in those early days of Ward L when each inmate sat in gloomy ilence.

"Here are a few examples taken from our eacher's report to illustrate what is done.

"F—— is a boy of twenty, whose spine is hopelessly injured. He cannot support his body at all, but lies on his bed resting on his elbows. In this position he has learned to knit wristlets and shawls, for which he finds a ready sale among the visitors. In the summer he lies flat on the grass and knits.

"E—— has locomotor ataxia, and is badly crippled. Our teacher asked one of our more experienced pupils to teach him how to knit, and now after several months of practice he makes fine white shawls which are ordered in advance by many people.

"W—— is a crippled bead-worker, who re-ports after a few months' absence a story of self-support during the summer from the sale of the bead-work which the teacher taught him to

"NO ATTEMPT AT SEGREGATION OF THESE
POOR UNFORTUNATE WRETCHES"

make. His bead chains were enough of a novelty to give him success. He said he lived comfortably on sixty cents a day.

"P—— spent the summer at Coney Island peddling baskets which we taught him to make; he was not so successful, but managed to sup-port himself until his return this fall.

"Work in the male blind ward of the Home for the Aged and Infirm on Blackwell's Island is progressing. Three blind men have learned to cane chairs, after long and patient efforts, and one of them hopes to make a living at chair caning. A fourth has learned to make baskets. In spite of the difficulty in teaching adult blind and the necessary slowness of the work we see already in this ward encouraging results of perseverance.

"Another blind man secured a small news-stand at the door of a restaurant, and is now successfully supporting himself.

"We have lately introduced light employment for the patients in one of the wards of the City Hospital, at the suggestion of a visiting doctor, who was anxious to try the curative effects of work upon the paralyzed women there. Since our teacher began with them last spring she re-ports several cases of improved physical con-dition, women with stiff and twisted hands having learned to crochet, and gradually to use all of their muscles. One of them is now regu-larly employed as nurses' messenger, and goes

THE FIRST MAN, LAME WITH RHEUMATISM,
NURSES HIS FELLOW INMATES

IN THE LIVING ROOM AT HEMPSTEAD—IDLING AWAY THE LONG WINTER'S DAY

up and down stairs quite readily. They are all delighted to have something to do, and are at work on the shawls which the Island Mission gives to each inmate at Christmas."

There is no reason why the inmates of almshouses should not be similarly employed.

Fifth, and finally, install the cottage system of buildings. That is, a number of small connected buildings, instead of one large building, with separate rooms for inmates instead of dormitories. This will make for privacy and decency and happiness, and friends or like-minded inmates may be housed together.

For instance, at Castleton Corners, Staten Island, when Homer Folks was Charity Commissioner of New York City in 1901–2, three large cottages were built—two for single women, the third for old married couples. Undoubtedly the inmates of these houses are the happiest in the State—the old couples ending their lives together in peace and security. It may be added, however, that the present Commissioner has seen fit to go back to the dormitory plan, and the eight new buildings being erected are of that type. The cottage system obtains in two or three other counties in the State.

This then, in short, is the plan—many features of which have been urged by the State Board of Charities and the State Charities Association for several years: Put the almshouses in charge of the State; drain them of improper inmates; put trained men at the head; do constructive work with the inmates and house them in cottages. This is modern, scientific, economical and humane, and only under such a plan may our almshouses be fit refuge for those of us too old to work, without friends and without money.

Index

Books in Abandoned History Series:

On the Edge of Town: Almshouses of Western New York
by Lynn S. Beman and Elizabeth Marotta

Dr. Skinner's Remarkable School for "Colored Deaf, Dumb, and Blind Children" 1857 – 1860
by James M. Boles, EdD, and Michael Boston, PhD

When There Were Poorhouses: Early Care in Rural New York 1808 – 1950
by James M. Boles, EdD

An Introduction to the British Invalid Carriage 1850 – 1978 by Stuart Cyphus

Abandoned Asylums of New England
A Photographic Journey by John Gray
Historical Insight by the Museum of disABILITY History

No Offense Intended: A Directory of Historical Disability Terms
by Natalie Kirisits, Douglas Platt and Thomas Stearns

The Gold Cure Institutes of Niagara Falls, New York 1890s by James M. Boles, EdD

Of Grave Importance: The Restoration of Institutional Cemeteries
by David Mack-Hardiman

They Did No Harm: Alternative Medicine in Niagara Falls, NY 1830–1930
by James M. Boles, EdD

Path to the Institution: The New York State Asylum for Idiots by Thomas E. Stearns

---

Children's Books Published by People Ink Press:

Ivan the Invacar Helps Big Dog, Written by Jim Boles, Illustrated by Bob Cunningham

Ivan the Invacar Helps Little Cat, Written by Jim Boles, Illustrated by Bob Cunningham

Ivan the Invacar and the Cave, Written by Jim Boles, Illustrated by Bob Cunningham

Ivan the Invacar Activity Book, Illustrated by Bob Cunningham

Ivan the Invacar Saves Wobbly Hubcap, Written by S. Boles, Illustrated by Bob Cunningham

---

Reprints from the Museum of disABILITY History Collection:

The Education of the Feeble-Minded by Kate Gannet Wells, Introduction by Douglas Platt

The Perkins Institution and Massachusetts School for the Blind
by Samuel Eliot, Introduction by Douglas Platt

Books can be purchased in person at the Museum of disABILITY History Store, located inside the Museum at 3826 Main Street, Buffalo NY. Questions? Give us a call at 716.629.3626.

Can't make it in to the store? Check out the Museum Store online at store.museumofdisability.org.

Most books are available to purchase online as E-books through Amazon (Kindle) and Barnes and Noble (Nook).

CPSIA information can be obtained
at www.ICGtesting.com
Printed in the USA
FFOW01n2020040216
20998FF